The Essential Guide to
Children's
Nutrition

ANGELA FALASCH[I]

Published in Great Britain in 2018 by
need2know
Remus House
Coltsfoot Drive
Peterborough
PE2 9BF
Telephone 01733 898103
www.need2knowbooks.co.uk

Contents

Help List 147

Introduction

Each generation changes but the results of good nutrition do not. Our reason for writing this book is that many parents and guardians are unsure how to encourage their children to eat healthily, and how to choose which foods to buy in the first place. It offers a comprehensive guide to the building blocks of a healthy diet, plus recipes that can be enjoyed by all the family. Our aim is not to dictate rules but to be a helping hand for anyone wanting to make the best food choices for their family.

Convenience meals, jars of baby food and takeaways offer a quick fix for time-poor parents and their children, but intensive farming practices and modern food preparation and preservation techniques mean that they can be inferior in nutritional value. Despite the reassuring face of a smiling cherub on the packaging of a bought baby purée or ready meals marketed at children, we believe these foods should be emergency standbys, not the basis of a child's diet.

Growing children (and their parents) should eat naturally prepared and simply cooked foods that are fresh, local and in season. The media, government, health organisations and food manufacturers are all debating these facts every day, yet it's still a challenge for families to access the information they need. Financially, physically and mentally, every single carer, child and family is unique. However, the nutrients that a body needs remain the same in every child and adult.

If you live or work with a child aged from birth to 18 years of age, whether you're a grandparent, guardian, teacher or parent, this book is for you. Today, we can browse for locally grown produce at farmers' markets, scan the shelves of our local stores and buy a huge range of organic goods: there is a greater choice of items on offer than ever before. Not all progress has been positive, however. We need to think about what all of these changes mean for the children in our lives. With hyperactivity, allergies, obesity and similar issues on the increase every single year, our children's food and lifestyles are vastly different from those of our own childhoods, and so is their health.

Nutritionist Angela Falaschi and writer Andréa Childs, who is a mother of two young children, present real-life, child and parent-friendly advice on how to choose, prepare, cook – and most importantly – enjoy food as a family. In today's economic climate, it's important that we're able to eat well on a relatively small budget, and this book sets out to prove that homemade meals don't have to be expensive. With an emphasis on the homemade, many of the recipes in this book have an Italian flavour inspired by the meals that Falaschi grew up with during her childhood in Italy. In recent years, scientists have concluded that the traditional Mediterranean diet promotes wellbeing for life, owing to its superb balance of nutrients. We hope that the positive, delicious changes that this book suggests will inspire you and your family to eat better, healthier and tastier food for years to come.

Disclaimer

Professional medical advice should not be replaced by this book, which is intended only for general information on childhood nutrition. It is strongly advised that you consult your child's healthcare professional before introducing changes to your child's diet, as the information in this book must be used alongside professional medical advice.

Note

In order to protect individuals' identities, all names in case studies have been changed.

A Beginner's Guide to Eating Right

Good Food for Children

What we eat feeds our bodies, but how we eat it nurtures our heart and soul. It's essential that mealtimes do not become battlegrounds. Many families eat the same, limited number of foods week in and week out and that can create nutritional imbalances that can be damaging for children and the adults that care for them. Whether you're a parent, carer, playgroup leader or teacher, providing healthy meals and teaching what makes a good diet is one of the ways you can protect and support the children you look after.

From vitamins for boosting immunity to infection to protein for healing and essential fatty acids for an evolving brain, every stage of a child's development makes fresh demands on their body. If you want your children to be strong, content, alert and healthy, it's essential that they have access to a good diet. It goes much further than that, however. In reducing their risk of developing conditions such as obesity, cancer, diabetes and heart disease, studies have found that proper nutrition in early childhood can have a massive impact on your child's chances at a long and healthy adulthood.

It also works the other way round. The risk of allergies, obesity, infections, skin conditions and juvenile-obset diabetes may be increased by a poor diet. Your child's risk of poor health both now and when they grow up can be increased if they're given foods that are high in salt, sugar and saturated fats. They also won't get to learn about how fantastic good food can make them feel, and will fail to develop a taste for healthy options. Unfortunately, there is also a lot of confusion about what "healthy" food actually is.

No one should underestimate the immense pressure that parents, carers, schools and nurseries face today. Schools, magazines and journals, health authorities and the government are all thankfully promoting the importance of good nutrition and the joys of eating, sharing and cooking good food. Providing all the nutrients that your child's growing body needs, creating meals that they love and helping them to develop a strong immune system doesn't need to be expensive or time-consuming, and this book aims to show you how.

'A good diet cannot guarantee good health for our children. But it is a vital first step.'

Quick Tip

Read food labels! Look for the words fructose, lactose, maltose, glucose, sucrose, syrup and molasses. There is hidden sugar in foods such as cereals, bars, processed foods, salad dressing, canned foods, cakes and yoghurt.

Food and Families

Sitting down at the table together will encourage your child to explore the tastes and textures of different foods, as they seek to eat what the grown-ups do. You'll be amazed at how your child's taste for healthy and delicious natural flavours develops if you involve them in preparing, selecting and cooking the food that you eat together. It's quite possibly the best way to avoid arguments, encourage your child to try new foods and make sure they actually eat what's put in front of them. Do not force your child to eat a meal you've prepared if they're refusing it. Your best option is to take it away and try to prepare and serve it differently the next time.

Celebrations wouldn't be the same without the food we share, so try to create occasions to eat with family and friends when possible. Your child will remember the conversations around the dinner table, not a television programme that was on in the background. Enjoy this time together, and keep the TV turned off. This will encourage your child to build strong relationships, and will provide happy memories of time with loved ones.

Eating Well on a Budget

It is true that the prices of certain foods, such as fresh fruit and vegetables, can seem expensive and that many people (and organisations such as schools and nurseries) have recently had to reduce their spending, meaning they can't afford to buy the food they would prefer for the children in their care. But feeding your family tasty, healthy meals doesn't have to cost more, however seductive the half price processed meals in the supermarket may be. You don't have to choose between eating well and spending less.

- Your child's physical, mental and emotional wellbeing can all be improved if you leave behind unhealthy options like sweets, fast food, fizzy drinks, burgers, chocolate and chips, and you won't believe how much money you'll save. These foods only ever leave people hungry and wanting more, anyway!

- Stay in control of your food budget by planning your meals in advance every week.

- How long can one meal feed your family? If you make a basic tomato sauce, it'll work with pasta one day and homemade pizza the next. Leftover cooked chicken can be mixed into salads or stir-fries for a brand new dish.

- Watching where food comes from and helping it grow will encourage your child to eat their harvest, so it's well worth growing your own vegetables and herbs if you can. They'll also be much cheaper than the ones you buy in a shop.

- You'll buy more than you need if you shop while hungry, so never shop on an empty stomach.

- Sprouting is also fun for children – seeds and pulses will grow very quickly sown on damp paper. Try sunflower, pumpkin, alfalfa or mung beans. Give them to your child as a nutrient-packed snack or sprinkle them into salads.

- Take advantage of two-for-the-price-of-one deals on foods like fresh berries – eat one punnet and freeze the other so you always have the ingredients for a vitamin-packed smoothie to hand.

- Eat low-cost vegetarian meals such as hot baked potatoes, delicious homemade soups and tasty bean casseroles, as well as more expensive meat and fish dishes.

- Remember that babies and toddlers generally eat what they are given and enjoy even bland flavours. This is the time to introduce healthy foods such as homemade vegetable and fruit purées, which cost a lot less than manufactured baby food and children's ready meals.

Food Additives

Some additives, although legal for use in foods here in the UK, are the cause of health concerns. Although it is accepted that eating too much salt or sugar may increase the risk of certain diseases, for example, salt and sugar are commonly used as preservatives. That said, the idea that all food additives are harmful is a myth. Some help maintain a food's nutritional value, preserve it to stop it from spoiling or aid in the preparation of the food.

However, some are used to disguise poor quality ingredients and inferior flavour, using artificial colourings and flavours to make the product seem more attractive.

According to the Food Standards Agency, certain additives may trigger a reaction in children and adults. If you believe your child may be reacting to an additive, read food labels carefully and consult your GP. A runny nose (rhinitis), asthma attack, urticaria (nettle rash), dermatitis or eczema may all occur as a result of these additives. Some additives have also been linked to hyperactivity in children.

(Source: Nutrition.org.uk, accessed 3 November 2018.)

Additives which are commonly believed to cause reactions include:

- Tartrazine (E102) – Sauces, soft drinks, cubed or powdered chicken broth and sweets all use this yellow colouring. Hyperactivity, urticaria, migraines, rhinitis and dermatitis have all been linked to the additive.

- Benzoates – These are found naturally in fruit and honey, but added artificially to mackerel and fruit juice products. In children, they can worsen symptoms of eczema and asthma. The Hyperactive Children's Support Group has put propyl 4-hydroxybenzoate (E216) on its exclusion list, though its use is still permitted.

- Sulphites, including sulphur dioxide – Used as a preservative in soft drinks, processed meat and dried vegetables. May cause asthma attacks.

Frozen Produce

Keep a few bags in the freezer for those days when the fruit and basket and vegetable box are bare. The speed with which frozen vegetables and fruit are picked and packaged helps to preserve vital nutrients, and can help busy parents to save their time and money.

Quick Tip

Give your child a few naturally sweet strawberries, raisins, sliced carrots, cherries or dried apricots as a snack to give them a taste for healthier treats while weaning them off sugary sweets.

The Problem of Poor Diet

It's not just the pleasure of sharing meals or the joy of tasting delicious food that is lost when cooking and dining becomes just another chore. The implications of limited, innutritious diets are greatest when meals are too often derived from heavily processed ingredients or come ready made from the freezer or chill cabinet, but this can also be an issue with fresh, home-cooked food if there isn't enough variation.

We (especially children) crave unhealthy options more because of the flavourings, stabilisers, thickeners, emulsifiers and preservatives that food manufacturers add to their products to make them more appealing to our eyes and taste buds. Some health professionals have raised questions about the long-term safety of food additives, as well as their immediate impact on child health and behaviour. The profit margins of the companies that produce them are boosted again, because all of these unhealthy additives will increase the shelf life of the foods.

'According to recent studies, foods high in salt, fat and sugar can cause changes in your child's brain chemistry that make them crave these foods more.'

Quick-Fix Diets and Limited Time

Here are a few tips to help keep your good intentions, so that you can shop, cook and eat in a way that's tasty, healthy and affordable, and won't have you slaving for hours in front of the cooker! Substituting home-cooked foods for cheap and easy (but not always nutritious) options at the dinner table – such as ready meals and takeaways – can become all too tempting when you're trying to juggle your home life, the demands of families and friends, your budget and your job. What children eat is essential for their health and happiness, and we're acutely aware of this as their carers and guardians.

- Stick to your shopping list. Make a plan for your week's meals ahead of time, and write down everything you need to buy. This means you won't order an expensive and greasy pizza because you've nothing in the fridge for dinner, and will save your money and time at the shops.

- Prepare lunch boxes the night before to cut down on the morning rush, leaving time for you and your child to enjoy a healthy breakfast.

- Freeze portions of healthy meals for when you're in a rush. Keep stocked up by preparing double quantities of things like soups, pastas, sauces and casseroles.

- Take advantage of late-night and Sunday opening at supermarkets – you will be able to think more clearly when the store is less busy, and take advantage of the price reductions on food at the end of the day or weekend.

- Buy fruit and vegetables every two days to ensure they're as fresh as possible. The rest of your groceries can be bought in a basic weekly or fortnightly shop.

- Keep a list of 20 or so favourite family meals and use them to plan weekly menus, swapping the mix around each time. Try to add in one new recipe each week, so you can introduce different nutrients and flavours.

Illnesses Tied to Unhealthy Foods

Even a healthy diet can trigger a reaction if a child is sensitive to a certain food. There can be links between what a child eats and specific ailments, as well as more general health complaints. A major step to ensuring your child's good health will be learning how you can manage and recognise these triggers.

Food Sensitivity

Food intolerances can develop when a food is eaten in large amounts. This means that if, for example, your child has toast for breakfast, sandwiches for lunch and pizza for dinner each day, they may develop an intolerance to wheat. Food sensitivity or intolerance can cause stomach pains, bloating, excess wind, constipation and diarrhoea, and contribute to conditions such as eczema, asthma and hay fever. Common problem foods include yeast, cow's milk, cheese, seeds, eggs, gluten (found in wheat and rye), corn, soya products (such as tofu and tempeh), peppers and aubergines.

Being sensitive to certain foods doesn't necessarily mean your child has an allergy. Eliminating these symptoms often involves figuring out which food or foods are causing the reaction and removing them from the diet for a while. In order to monitor any problems, it's often a good idea to restrict potentially problematic foods until your child is about a year old, and then to introduce them gradually.

Keep a food diary of what your child eats for a week if you think they might have an intolerance to a certain food. Before eating the same food again, leave a three-day gap to allow symptoms to develop (unless you've noticed that your child has a problem with them, don't apply this rule to vegetables or fruit). If your child has a delayed reaction to eating a certain food, this gap will allow you to find it. Consult your GP or a nutritionist if you want more advice about food intolerances.

Allergic Reactions

The number of children suffering food allergies has really exploded in recent years. While scientists are unsure about some of the reasons for this rise, it is known that having a close family member who suffers from an allergy, including food allergies, hay fever, eczema and asthma, increases a child's risk of developing an allergic condition, although it might be different to that suffered by their parents and siblings. Eczema, hay fever, asthma and other allergic conditions are also on the rise.

- Talk to an allergy specialist, your GP or health visitor if you think your child may be at risk from allergies or are concerned about feeding them safely.

- Monitor your child's reactions if you know that you're allergic to a certain food by giving them a small amount unmixed with other foods.

- Make sure an allergic child's diet is rich in vitamin C, essential fatty acids (if fish is not the problem), beta carotene (which the body converts into vitamin A), magnesium (important for muscles, nerves and the metabolism of calcium), calcium (for strong bones and teeth) and zinc (essential for growth and development).

- Common allergens include milk, eggs, nuts, fruit, soya, wheat, fish and shellfish.

Healthy Weight and Obesity

If you are concerned about your child's weight, the first step is to get a proper assessment from a GP or health professional. It's also worth looking at your child's (and the family's) lifestyle – how much sugary, fatty, or processed foods do you eat?

What activities are you involved in? Planning activities as a family, such as bike rides, sport activities, or just games in the park, can also boost fitness levels for you and your child, helping to overcome any weight problems.

Quick Tip

Foods with shorter lists of ingredients are generally the healthier options. Check food labels for added sugar, salt, additives and saturated fats.

It can be hard for a concerned parent or carer to know whether a child's dimples are "baby fat" or a sign that they're overweight amid all of the government warnings, unhealthy food advertisements and sensational headlines, but it's an unavoidable fact that childhood obesity is on the increase. Your doctor can investigate if there's an underlying health problem and look at their body fat percentage in relation to their age and height to give you a clearer picture of how healthy your child is. They will recommend that your child gets five daily portions of fruit and vegetables. Try to involve your child in making these decisions about healthier food choices, as working together to come to these decisions about your weekly meals is a great way to explain how important a healthy diet can be. We'll discuss obesity in greater detail in Chapter Six.

Eat the Seasons

Local and farmers' markets are a great way to buy fresh at a reasonable price, and your child will love the colour and bustle of the stalls. It's far better to eat strawberries that are grown in Britain in the summertime, fed by natural sunshine, soil and rainwater, than those that are flown thousands of food miles in the winter, nurtured under artificial light and in heated polytunnels and fed with artificial fertilisers. When buying fresh produce, always choose shops where the stock moves fast, so you can be sure the food has not been there a long time.

There's no better way for your child to get the vitamins and minerals, fibre and carbohydrates they need than by eating the freshest vegetables and fruits, which are packed full of nutrients. Another guarantee of flavour and quality is to eat foods in the season they'd naturally grow, and avoid those that have been grown artificially just so the shops can stock them all year. There are no coincidences in nature. Fresh salads appear in the summer when we crave light and fresh raw foods, hedgerows fill with blackberries that are rich in vitamin C just as our bodies prepare for autumn, and as soon as we begin to need comforting energy in the winter, starchy vegetables begin to thrive.

Eating this way will help your child to understand nature's perfect rhythms and the ways in which our bodies have evolved to work with them. Check that the vegetables and fruits you choose aren't battered, tired-looking or limp, as these are all signs that they've been on the shelves and away from the fields for too long. Good greengrocers and supermarkets should not have these issues, as they'll have a faster turnover on their fresh foods.

The different colours of fresh produce indicate the varying nutrients they contain, so ask your child if they can find vegetables of all the colours of the rainbow to bring home. This is a great way of getting your child involved in picking healthier foods.

Organic Foods

It may not be possible to give your child a totally organic diet, but buying some naturally produced meat, fruit, vegetables and dairy products is a great start. The benefits of eating organic for your child are that they generally contain more nutrients than food that has been intensively cultivated and they are free from growth hormones, pesticides and other chemicals that are used in conventional farming. Organic foods do tend to be more expensive than non-organic options, though their price has dropped significantly thanks to increases in both supply and demand.

People are beginning to understand that apples, for example, will be more nutritious if they're allowed to grow and ripen naturally than if they're sprayed with insecticides and pesticides and harvested before they're even fully ripe. One of the most important steps that you can make for your child's health, now and in the future, is to serve them a wide variety of fresh foods – even if buying organic isn't an option for you.

Summing Up

- Your child's lifelong eating patterns can be established by what they eat as a child.

- Now and in the future, your child might experience health problems if their diet is too high in processed foods, sugar, saturated fats, salt and artificial additives.

- Your shopping basket should be full of seasonal fresh foods.

- Your child can pick up positive associations with food if you eat with family and friends.

- Involving your child in planning and cooking meals can encourage healthy eating.

- Planning healthy meals in advance can save you time, stress and money.

- A well-balanced diet that is rich in nutrients can help to prevent health problems in both childhood and adulthood.

2

The Nutrients Your Child Needs

Water, carbohydrates, fats, minerals, vitamins and proteins are the six main categories of nutrients that your child needs to be getting. These all work together like one big team, combining their unique qualities to reach their vital goal of better health.

- The nutrients that we need in smaller quantities, such as vitamins, minerals and trace minerals, are called micronutrients.

- Water, carbohydrates, fats and proteins are all needed by our body every day in fairly large amounts. We call this type of nutrient, "macronutrients".

Micronutrients

Minerals and Vitamins

Vitamins and minerals are the workers behind the scene in a balanced diet, helping to keep the body in tune. It's essential that your child's diet has a plentiful and balanced supply. They can be either fat soluble or water soluble. They detoxify the body of harmful chemicals and keep our immune system in top condition. The ways our children think about food will be transformed if we give them all the information they need about vitamins and minerals. Vitamins and minerals are found in almost all fresh foods.

We give them green vegetables because they're rich in iron and oranges because they're full of vitamin C, but there's more to it than that. They can reduce allergy symptoms in the summer and ward off colds in the winter. They're magical, natural medicines that can be taken whenever they're needed. They work with other nutrients and also with one another. There are around 20 vitamins that we currently know. From keeping our skin, eyes, lungs, bones and muscles all functioning efficiently to converting glucose into energy, these vitamins are essential in thousands of different body processes. How much you need of each depends on age, sex, health and lifestyle. Not getting enough of these vital nutrients can lead to a range of different ailments, but equal damage can occur if we get too much.

Fat-Soluble Vitamins	
Vitamin A	Find it in veal, milk, egg yolk, spinach, broccoli and all orange and yellow fruits and vegetables. Wellbeing and beauty are connected with this vitamin. Its benefits include skin health, an improved immune system and night vision.
Vitamin D	Fortified cheeses, butter and margarine, fish oils and egg yolk are all great sources of vitamin D, as is exposure to sunlight. Healthy bones and teeth rely on this vitamin as it allows the body to absorb calcium.
Vitamin E	Dietary sources include vegetable oils, leafy greens and nuts. All cell membranes are protected by this powerful antioxidant. Poultry and eggs also contain a small amount of vitamin E.
Vitamin K	This vitamin helps with the formation of tissues and allows blood to clot. Find it in egg yolk, meat and dark green vegetables.

Water-Soluble Vitamins	
Vitamin B	They are important for the nervous system and are needed in the process of releasing energy from carbohydrates, proteins and fats. Find them in whole grains, beans, seeds, nuts, meat, fish, eggs and other proteins.
Vitamin C	This important vitamin helps to boost immunity and can be found in fresh vegetables and fruit.

Should Your Child Be Taking Supplements?

It may be that a vitamin and mineral supplement could be beneficial to your child's health, especially if they don't yet eat a wide range of foods. Your child would obtain all the vitamins they need from their diet if this were an ideal world. Sadly, though, the food we harvest and consume is less nutrient-rich than it once was, as intensive farming methods have depleted the soil of nutrients. They are depleted of goodness, and so are processed foods. For advice on what supplements your child may need, and on which are the most easily absorbed by the body, you should consult your GP or a nutritionist.

Minerals	
Calcium	Calcium is found in milk, dairy products, root vegetables, seeds and some nuts. Foods that interfere with absorption of calcium include spinach, sugary foods and rhubarb. Your child should not be eating these foods in excess. Calcium keeps teeth and bones strong. To maximise its absorption, it should be eaten with magnesium-rich foods (see below).
Iron	Leafy vegetables, lentils, oatmeal, raisins, egg yolk, dried beans, prunes and dried peaches are all great sources of the trace element iron. We need this in order to form red blood cells.
Magnesium	Good sources include leafy green vegetables, wholegrain cereals, nuts, seeds, beans and soya milk. Magnesium is very important for muscles and nerves, and functions alongside calcium. The mineral also helps to release energy from proteins, fat and carbohydrates by working with B vitamins.
Potassium	Helps to maintain the body's acid-alkaline balance. Many vegetables and fruits, especially bananas, are great sources of potassium. It's important to make sure your child eats plenty of fresh produce as deficiency can be found in the young.
Sodium	Essential for nerve and muscle functioning and to regulate the body's fluid balance. Salt in foods is the main way we take in sodium. Heart problems, high blood pressure and imbalances of other minerals may become issues if we take too much sodium.
Zinc	Best sources include seafood, red meat, nuts, seeds, pulses and wholegrains. Immune resistance, mental function and hormone production all rely on the trace element zinc.

Macronutrients

Fats

Fat is actually essential for the health of your child's body, however concerned the parents and carers around you are about the amount of fat that their children eat.

- It protects the internal organs and provides high energy and insulation.

- It allows vitamins A, D, E and K to travel around your body.

- It makes our food taste better.

- It helps to regulate enzymes and produce prostaglandins (hormone-like substances that are essential for many body processes).

- It helps to form cell membranes and the myelin sheath essential to the function of the nervous system.

What's important is the type of fat your child eats. Needless to say, your child isn't going to experience good health now or when they grow up if they're living on chocolate and chips.

- Butter, meat, milk and other animal products contain saturated fats. These should be eaten in small quantities, as they've been linked to obesity and conditions like heart disease.

- Polyunsaturated fats come from vegetable sources, such as plant oils, nuts and seeds. These provide vital nutrients called "essential fatty acids" and the body cannot make them itself so they're essential to our diet.

Essential Fatty Acids

These types of fat are good for building the body's cells, especially those of the brain and nervous system – essential in a developing child. Omega 3 (also known as LNA or linolenic acid) and omega 6 (also known as LA or linoleic acid) are the two essential fatty acids.

- Wheat germ, hemp, sunflower oil, corn, soya bean, safflower oil and pumpkin seeds are all good sources of omega 6. The richest source of omega 6 is safflower.

- Omega 3: good sources include oily fish such as herring, salmon, sardines and fresh tuna, as well as flaxseed (also known as linseed). Flaxseeds contain the most omega 3.

Angela's Case Study: Siblings with Asthma

Charlie wanted to make sure that his four children (aged 2, 4, 7 and 12) were eating a balanced diet, so he came to see me. Asthma ran in his family and affected the two oldest children, who also had acne.

Their vegetable intake was limited – tomatoes, cucumber and, sometimes, broccoli. They all loved fried foods, including fish and chips, and ate a large number of burgers. I discovered that the children loved processed cheese sandwiches and were eating far too many dairy products, especially the two eldest. Every day, the children were eating chocolate, biscuits and sweets.

I felt the amount of saturated fat and sugar in their diet was contributing to their acne. The older children's already delicate respiratory systems were being impaired by the mucous formed by the dairy foods they were eating.

I advised Charlie to give his children a teaspoon of Udo's Oil, which is rich in omega 3, 6 and 9, daily, or to sprinkle it on their cold food. I also asked him to increase the essential fatty acids in their diet by increasing the children's intake of oily fish. Finally, I stressed that the children should drink more water, to help eliminate toxins. Charlie promised that he would help balance their nutritional intake by giving them a wider range of foods.

After a month, the children were suffering from fewer asthma attacks and had much clearer skin.

Good Grains

There are lots of different whole grains that can provide different nutrients and flavours for your child, other than the wheat that fills our diet here in the UK (and the West in general).

- Buckwheat is actually a seed, but it has all the great nutrients that you can expect from any whole grain and its flour works perfectly as a whole grain flour replacement. It's very high in B vitamins, fibre, magnesium and rutin. Have a go at eating it in homemade pancake or noodles.

- Quinoa can now be bought in most supermarkets and is very affordable. It's full of B vitamins and fibre. Quinoa is perfect for coeliacs and people with a gluten intolerance or sensitivity as it's completely gluten-free. Try eating it instead of rice with your dinner tonight!

- Corn – rich in some B vitamins, high in fibre, beta carotene and vitamin C. Homemade popcorn, made without oil, is a great alternative to crisps for your child.

Carbs

Carbohydrates are broken down into a sugar called glucose in the body, providing the fuel that your child needs for a day of growing, playing and learning. Sugar and honey; grains like rice and oats; pulses like lentils, chickpeas and beans; some root vegetables; pasta, cakes and pastries are all rich in carbohydrates.

Complex Carbohydrates

'Very few children don't like pasta. Choose wholegrain varieties, which are rich in B vitamins, and their bodies will love it, too.'

Complex carbohydrates are found in wholegrains, wholemeal flour, wild rice and whole oats, pulses and some vegetables. Energy is released at a steady pace and lasts for a long period of time when your child eats these carbohydrates, which are made from polysaccharides (long chains of sugar) which are digested very slowly. The fibre they contain will prevent overeating by helping your child to feel fuller for longer, and they're packed with vital nutrients.

Simple Carbohydrates

Quick Tip

It's generally best to avoid giving too many simple carbohydrates to your child, but a snack like a biscuit or fruit smoothie, which can release energy quickly, can be just the between-meals boost they need after sport or playtime at the park.

- Simple carbohydrates lead to a rapid rise in the amount of glucose in your child's blood as the body can digest them easily. Their energy is released very quickly, but is also used up quickly so they won't stave off hunger for so long.

- Poor health can be a consequence of the consumption of large amounts of refined carbohydrates over time, especially white sugar (sucrose).

- White flour is used to make white bread, cakes and pastries. As well as reducing the nutrient content of flour, the refining process cuts down the amount of fibre and creates easily digestible "double sugars", making these foods easy to digest and creating a surge of sugar in the body after eating.

Protein

Protein requirements rise during periods of fast growth, including infancy, so it's essential that your child eats at least two portions of protein each day. Essential for the growth and repair of every single cell in your child's body, proteins are basically the building blocks that keep your body alive.

- They're broken down into smaller units called amino acids when digested by special acids in the stomach.

- Seeds, meat, fish, cheese, soy, nuts, eggs, milk and poultry are just some of the the protein-rich foods that should be included in your child's diet.

- The body cannot store proteins. Excess amounts are converted into energy and fat.

- Around 20 amino acids are required by the body to make the various types of protein. Each of these amino acids (nine in children) must be supplied by the diet. These are known as "essential amino acids".

How Much Protein Is Needed?

Vegetarians and vegans must select foods that complement one another and eat them in the same meal in order to obtain all of the essential amino acids they need. Plant foods lack some amino acids and are therefore called "incomplete". For example, legumes such as beans are deficient in the amino acids methionine and cysteine, but rich in lysine. "Complete" proteins, which contain all of the nine essential amino acids, are found in proteins from animal sources. A variety of protein foods should make up your child's diet.

A mix of essential amino acids, as well as the perfect balance of flavours, can all be found in one meal if you include certain combinations of complementary foods. You won't find any lysine in seeds, nuts or grains, though they are rich in methionine and cysteine. You'll find all of the essential amino acids your child needs if you combine your seeds, nuts or grains with legumes, which have plenty of lysine. Try, for example, a portion of rice with a vegetable chilli rich in kidney beans.

'Give protein and carbohydrates together in the same meal. Fibre from the carbohydrates will aid digestion, and the protein will help energy to be released more slowly and last longer, so your child won't feel hungry soon after eating.'

Angela's Case Study: The Vegetarian Child

Anna's three-year-old daughter was underweight and prone to skin infections, so she brought her to see me. The child, Bea, ate mainly pizza, pasta and white bread sandwiches, and both mother and daughter followed a vegetarian diet, so I quickly realised that the little girl's diet was lacking in protein when I saw her food diary.

I suggested she eat fruit such as mango and papaya, which boost skin health. It's advisable for vegetarian children to eat some milk, eggs or cheese to complement the missing proteins in plants. I helped Anna to understand that all of the refined carbohydrates in Bea's diet were suppressing her appetite for other foods. They were causing her intestinal flora to become imbalanced, contributing to her pimples, so it was important to cut down on these foods.

'Brown bread looks like wholewheat but the colour comes from additives. It's no better than white loaves.'

I recommended a diet rich in soya beans, whole grains, nuts, seeds and wheat germ. As Anna and Bea didn't eat fish or meat, they needed to choose other foods that would provide complete proteins when combined as a meal. Rice with lentils or tofu; legumes and grains, which supplement each others' missing amino acids; peanut butter on whole grain toast; and hummus, which is a complete protein thanks to its combination of sesame seeds and chickpeas, were also good additions to the menu.

Six weeks later, Anna came back to see me. Bea's skin was much clearer, and she'd managed to put on 2kg in weight.

Staying Hydrated

Children especially need to top up their fluid levels frequently, as they are generally more active and have a faster metabolism than adults. As we need large quantities in our diet, water, just like proteins, fats and carbohydrates, can be classed as a macronutrient.

Which Foods Should I Cut Down On?

The good thing is that by adding more nutrient-rich choices to your family's meals, there will automatically be less space on the table (and in your child's tummy) for poorer options. You know what foods you need to give to your child by now, and which elements are necessary to make up a good diet. Moderation is also important though, and there are some foods you should only be eating in small amounts.

- White bread – even "enriched" versions won't contain all the goodness of wholegrain versions. All of the good nutrients are stripped away from white flour and bread products long before they get to you.

- Chocolate and sweeties – sweets and chocolate are high in sugar. While no parent should deny their child the occasional treat, the refined carbohydrates in sweets and chocolate have no nutritional value and can cause real damage to your child's teeth or suppress their immune system by upsetting their intestinal flora. Like cakes and biscuits, chocolate often contains hydrogenated fat. However, less sugar and fat will be found in good chocolate that contains around 70% cocoa solids or more.

- Salt – 75% of the salt we eat comes from processed foods. Some labels will list it simply as "sodium", and you're likely to find it in things like sausages, bacon, ready meals, takeaways, snacks, ham and crisps. High blood pressure has been linked to excess salt, which can also cause stress on the adrenal glands and kidneys.

- Processed meat – these are low in nutrients and high in nitrates (used as a preservative and linked to an increased risk of colon cancer), saturated fats and salt. Lots of kids love things like sausages, sliced ham, bacon and burgers, but it may be worth cutting down if you can.

- Fizzy drinks – these can be high in artificial flavourings, preservatives and colouring. The carbon dioxide and phosphoric acid used to make them fizz can inhibit absorption of calcium.

- Cakes and biscuits – partially hydrogenated fats (also known as trans fats) are found mainly in bought biscuits and cakes. They have been found to raise cholesterol and increase risk of heart disease.

- High-fibre cereal – while some fibre is essential in the diet for efficient digestion, too much can cause a deficiency of important minerals including calcium, iron, and zinc.

Salt targets for children have been set out by the Food Standards Agency:

- 1 to 3 years – 2g salt a day (0.8g sodium)

- 4 to 6 years – 3g salt a day (1.2g sodium)

- 7 to 10 years – 5g salt a day (2g sodium)

- 11 years and over – 6g salt a day (2.4g sodium)

(Source: www.nhs.uk, accessed 3 November 2018.)

'Foods containing the following additives must be labelled 'may have an adverse effect on activity and attention in children – Tartrazine (E102), Quinoline Yellow (E104), Sunset Yellow (E110), Carmosine (E122), Ponceau 4R (E124), Allura Red (E129) and Sodium Benzoate.'

Summing Up

- Water, carbohydrates, fats, minerals, vitamins and proteins are the six main nutrients that we need in our diets.

- The body's cells are unable to grow or repair themselves without protein. Amino acids are formed when the body breaks it down.

- While some fats are linked with health problems, others are essential for many body processes.

- To promote good health and development, certain foods should be reduced in your child's diet.

- Some food additives can trigger reactions such as asthma, eczema and hyperactivity in children.

- Vitamins and minerals are micronutrients essential to keep the body healthy.

- Animal proteins contain all the amino acids your child needs. Vegetable proteins are incomplete and must be combined in order to supply the full range of amino acids.

- Simple carbohydrates release energy quickly. Complex carbohydrates are higher in nutrients and will help your child to feel fuller for longer.

3

The First Year

One of the most frustrating, joyful, messy and enjoyable things you can do with your child is to feed them their first foods. There may be days when your lovingly pulped purée is speedily spat out, or you seem to spend more time picking peas off the floor than you do watching them being swallowed. This is when you establish how your family enjoys and shares mealtimes, and signals the start of a lifelong relationship between your child and their food. Not only are you guaranteeing that your child eats a good range of nutrients from ingredients you have chosen yourself, but you're developing their taste for a wide range of flavours, textures and smells – all of which will help your child to savour food as they grow up and make them less picky about the choices put in front of them.

This challenge will be approached by every child a little differently. One may quickly develop a taste for vegetables, another may eat them only when sweetened with pear or apple. While one child will reject all cutlery in favour of fingers, another will be more than happy to eat theirs with a spoon.

It won't always be easy to encourage your child to eat, and we're not here to pretend it will. All the same, it's well worth it to make your own baby foods when you can, and eventually to prepare dishes that the whole family can enjoy – from the eldest to the youngest. We promise, those jars of baby food in the shops won't look so appealing when you see how easy, fun and inexpensive it is to rustle up your own child- and health-friendly dishes.

All you can really do is go for it. Invest in a plastic mat for under the table, and embrace the challenge ahead of you.

Q & A – Water and Other Drinks

You'll need to introduce your child to new drinks, too, not just new foods. Here are some of the basics:

Should I Use a Bottle or a Cup?

It's a good idea to introduce the idea of using a cup as they move on from exclusively drinking milk – they'll need to learn to give up the bottle and sip from a cup at some point, so why not start now? For that, start by putting just a mouthful of water into the bottom of a one- or two-handled cup, hold it to their lips and pour a few drops into their mouth. Allow your child to swallow, then give them more water until they don't want any more. If your child resists drinking this way, leave it for a couple of weeks then try again. Cups with spouts won't teach your child to drink properly, though they're very handy for when you're out and about. With enough practice, they should be able to drink from a regular cup and spill less than they swallow.

Is it Okay to Give My Baby Tap Water?

If your child is younger than six months old, you'll need to boil and cool tap water before you give it to them. So long as you do this, it'll be fine. Babies shouldn't drink certain bottled waters, as they can be unsafe due to the high amount of minerals they contain. Even if your bottled water has been labelled as safe for babies, it won't be sterile. If your baby is below six months of age, the water will need to be boiled and cooled, just like tap water.

What about Other Drinks?

The best drinks for your child are milk, water and a tiny amount of juice. Harmful additives such as sweeteners, colourings and flavourings make up a big part of other drinks like fizzy pop and diluted squash, and these don't really have any nutritional value.

Does My Baby Need to Drink?

Until they reach six months of age, additional drinks for your child aren't really an issue. Formula-fed babies can be given a little boiled and cooled water. As breast milk will naturally meet all their food and hydration needs, babies who are being breastfed won't really need any extra fluids – not even water. Don't let your child's fluid intake drop when you decrease the amount of milk you give them at six months. Use diluted fruit juices and water to make up the difference.

Do I Need a Water Filter?

Your child may prefer filtered tap water in hard water areas, as the process can improve its taste. Chlorine, dirt, lead and other potentially harmful materials can also be removed from the water through the use of filters. Filtered water will still need to be boiled, however.

Is Juice Safe for Babies?

Lots of great nutrients like vitamins, minerals and enzymes are packed into freshly made fruit and vegetable juices, and these are a great way to introduce a baby to new flavours. Too much juice can reduce their appetite for milk and cause diarrhoea, stomach cramps and tooth decay. Breast or formula milk should be your child's main drink for the first year, so make sure any juices you give are diluted and only given in small amounts. Stomach upsets can become a big problem if your child has acidic juices like orange and grapefruit, so avoid these.

Portion Sizes

Your child's appetite will gradually increase once they get used to eating more than just milk, and you can gradually move from feeding them around 50g each meal right up to 300g, boosting their portion sizes just a little each time. Their body will tell them naturally when they have had enough to eat, so don't ask them to finish their bowlful if it's obvious that they don't want it. When your child is just starting on solid foods, they should each day be having around three feeds of milk (either formula or breast).

How to Prepare Purées

- Steam your child's fruits and vegetables, as this will reserve as many nutrients as possible while making it possible to soften them enough for your child's first mouthfuls. If steaming isn't an option, you can boil them in a small amount of water.

- Use a food processor, blender, or mouli to mask them into a smooth purée – add a little of the cooking water to thin, if necessary.

- You'll be able to introduce more texture into your child's meals as they grow teeth and get better at eating. At this stage, fruit can be grated or puréed raw, and vegetables can be lightly cooked and given as finger food or mashed only roughly.

Don't Start Solids Too Early

The first time your child begins to crawl, laughs at something or claps their hands is exciting. Giving your child that first spoonful of baby rice is just as thrilling, which is why it's tempting to start them on solids sooner than is necessary. With new babies, every milestone is an exciting event. Waiting, however, is a good idea for a number of reasons. There's no evidence to suggest that giving your child solid foods before the age of six months has any health advantage, as milk will supply all of their nutritional needs until then.

- Most children can only use their lips to take food from the spoon, chew it, and use their tongue to move it to the back of their mouth from six months onwards. They may be able to sit up, take in and swallow puréed foods from five months, but they won't be actively eating.

- Especially if there's a history of allergy in the family, introducing solids before six months can increase their risk of infection and the developments of allergies like eczema and asthma. At six months, your child's gut and kidneys will have matured enough to cope better with a broader diet.

- There's no evidence that waiting until six months will affect your child's ability to chew or make them more likely to be a fussy eater.

- At this age your child will have sufficient hand-eye coordination to pick up finger foods, and will be curious to try new tastes and textures.

Baby's First Food: Milk

You're probably already thinking about moving your child on from a diet of only milk to one that includes things like vegetables and fruits – and eventually pulses, meat, fish, fats and dairy products – by the time you'll read this book. It's never too late to start paying attention to your child's nutrition, though it's worth starting from birth if possible.

Formula Milk

You can consult a GP, nutritionist or dietitian about the best formula for your child. A range of nutrients to help your child grow and develop can now be found in milk formulas, which are developed to be as close to human milk as possible. So if you choose not to breastfeed or are unable to do so for medical reasons, don't worry!

Breastfeeding

For the first year of life, the World Health Organisation (WHO) and the government recommend that milk makes up an important part of your child's diet. They believe that breastfeeding is healthier than bottle-feeding with formula milk, and that your child should only be fed with milk (formula or breast) and nothing more for the first six months. Alongside breast or formula milk, solid foods can gradually be introduced from six months onwards. This is for a number of reasons:

- For the first six months of life, according to research compiled by the NHS and WHO, breast milk can provide all the nutrients that a baby needs for healthy growth and development.

- Ear infection, conjunctivitis and respiratory infection, along with a range of other infections, can be protected against by the protective factors found in breastmilk. (Source: **www.nhs.uk**, accessed 5 November 2018.)

- Even if breastfeeding isn't a long-term option for whatever reason, feeding your child this way for the first few days after birth, when a mother's body naturally produced antibody-rich colostrum, can boost your child's immunity and may help to prevent future illnesses.

- The combination of nutrients in breast milk naturally changes as your child grows.

Signs Your Baby Is Ready for Solids

Each child is individual and may not fit the averaged results from research conducted on thousands of babies, but as a general rule the NHS and WHO both recommend waiting until six months before starting your child on solid foods. Your child is most likely ready to expand their diet and move beyond the world of milk if they exhibit these signs:

- They don't need support to sit up.
- They're reaching and trying to grab your food.
- They no longer have a tongue-thrust reflex. (You can test this by preparing some baby rice and feeding your child a small portion. They aren't yet ready for spoon-feeding if they're still pushing it out of their mouth with their tongue after several attempts.)
- They are picking up and tasting finger foods.
- They are taking an interest in what the rest of the family is eating.

Cow Milk

From the age of one, cow's milk should ideally be introduced to your baby. It contains insufficient iron or vitamins C and D for their needs until then, so it shouldn't be given as their sole source of milk.

Don't Put Off Solid Foods for Too Long

Your child needs to replenish the stores of iron and other essential nutrients that they built up before birth, so it's not advisable to wait more than six months to wean them. Unwanted stress at the dinner table may also become an issue for you and your child if you delay their introduction to the tastes and textures of foods, as it can make eating solids more of a challenge.

Cooking Safely

Here are a few tips to help you avoid food poisoning for you and your child. It's vital that you cook with food safety in mind.

- Avoid contamination by keeping raw and cooked meats separate from each other in the fridge.

- Use hot soapy water to wash all bowls, tupperware pots and cooking equipment, and rinse off the suds. Use a clean tea towel to dry or allow to air dry.

- As soon as it is cool, refrigerate or freeze any cooked food you aren't eating right away.

- Only put as much food as you think your child will eat, then top up if necessary. Don't save any food left in the bowl for a later meal – saliva transferred from your child's mouth to the food by the spoon will begin to digest the food and it may start to go off.

- Keep work surfaces and chopping boards clean.

- Wash your hands with soap and water before preparing food and again if you touch raw meat, fish or eggs, which can carry bacteria. Make sure your hands are clean before feeding your child.

'Never leave your child alone while they eat because of the risk of choking.'

Weaning (Six to Seven Months)

What will your child's first solid food be when the big day finally arrives? Although it's exciting to tick off all the new foods that your child will eat, it's important to introduce each item individually and give it exclusively for two or three days, so that you can be sure it doesn't cause a reaction. Many parents find baby rice to be a suitable option as its bland flavour won't be too far different from that of the milk your child is used to, and it's easily digested by most babies.

Don't worry if your child seems to find it difficult to swallow this new food at first. Make just a teaspoon or two at first, and keep the consistency nice and runny ("solid" is a bit of a strong word for foods at this age) by thinning it out with milk or boiled and cooled water. After a few days, try introducing a single-variety fruit or vegetable purée. It may take a day or two to learn how to use their tongue to bring food to the back of their mouth, as they're still only accustomed to drinking milk.

Your baby may be tempted by a spoonful of puréed apple and pear, as babies tend to have a sweet tooth. However, you don't want your child to reject vegetables because they'd rather have fruit, so it may be a better idea to opt for a naturally sweet vegetable like carrot or parsnip instead.

Signs that your child may be sensitive to the food you're giving them may include excessive wind, vomiting, a rash around the bottom or mouth, waking in the night, watering eyes or a runny nose and diarrhoea. If this happens, leave the food out of your child's diet for a few weeks before making a second attempt. If they continue to have adverse reactions, don't feed your child the food again until they're at least a year old.

Doing It for Themselves

Once solid foods are on the menu, it's more than likely that a set of sticky fingers will begin to grab and prod the food in your baby's bowl, or attempt to steal the spoon you're trying to feed them with. Don't discourage self-feeding, however messy it gets. If your child is to learn to feed themselves properly, they'll need to go through this vital developmental step.

- Keep mealtimes from becoming a fight over cutlery by giving your child a spoon identical to the one you're holding.

- Keep your child interested at the table by providing a variety of soft foods that they can eat with their hands. Good options include chunks of peeled fruit like banana and orange, small cubes of cheese, pieces of wholemeal toast and steamed vegetables like broccoli or potato.

- Let your child play with their food, within reason. Exploring the feel of food is the first step to a love of food and healthy eating.

Reheating and Storing Foods

- For feeds during the day, freshly cooked vegetables and fruit can be cooled and kept in the fridge.

- To make your life simpler, cook more than you need and freeze the excess in ice cube trays.

- Once the cubes freeze, you can put them in bags, label them and keep them in the freezer.

- Take out the cubes you need for the day's meals in the morning, put them in bowls and store them in the fridge until it's time to feed your baby. They'll take around an hour to defrost.

- You can can put the bowl on a larger bowl of hot water to warm them gently, or take them out half an hour before use to let them warm to room temperature.

Quick Tip

Until your child is one year old, they shouldn't be eating honey. It can make babies very ill, as some batches contain a bacteria called Clostridium botulinum.

Bringing in Proteins (Seven to Nine Months)

You can begin to add more texture, nutrients and flavours to your child's diet once they're used to eating. You will still need to purée these foods at first, increasing the chunkiness as your child gets better at chewing and swallowing. Iron is important for your child now as babies are born with a store that lasts for around six months. Look for foods that are rich in protein and iron, such as fish (especially oily varieties, and not shellfish), eggs and poultry. Iron deficiency is not easy to spot, so you need to give them food that will replenish their supplies.

For a mini but balanced meal, mix purées with vegetables and carbohydrates like pasta and wholemeal bread.

Great First Foods – Seven to Nine Months

- Spinach and other leafy dark-green vegetables;
- Well-cooked or hard-boiled eggs;
- Finger foods – pasta, raw and cooked vegetables, fruit;
- Turkey.

Foods to Avoid:

- Cheese (soft, unpasteurised and blue cheeses should be avoided for the first year due to a risk of listeria);
- Nuts (until one year; five if there is a family history of allergy);
- Shellfish (until nine months; this is a major cause of food poisoning and may trigger allergies);
- Honey (until one year).

Nine to 12 Months – Family Meals

Your child's daily menu should now look like yours, with three main meals a day – breakfast, lunch and dinner – plus a few healthy snacks and plenty of water to drink. Your child's appetite will be growing as they do, so you might want to give them two courses at lunch and dinner – fruit, fromage frais and yoghurt make great puddings. Mealtimes become simpler, cheaper, and a real shared experience at this stage, as you should be able to give your child at least some of the food that you cook for the rest of the family.

Just make sure you spoon out your child's portion before adding any salt or sugar to the dish. If necessary, you can still grate, squash or chop your child's food, but you should be able to (finally!) retire the blender.

The Building Blocks of a Healthy Diet

Encourage your child to eat a wide range of different foods. Don't be scared to give your child stronger flavours such as garlic, herbs and spices. The vitamins and minerals they need aren't all found in white bread! This may also stop them from becoming fussy eaters later on, as they'll be introduced early to lots of different flavours.

- Suitable protein sources might include softly-cooked meat, eggs, beans and fish – give your child one or two of these each day.

- At every meal and as snacks, your child should be getting plenty of fruit and vegetables.

- Every day at this age, they will still need around 600ml of formula or breast milk.

- Make sure your child eats dairy foods such as cheese, fromage frais and yoghurt.

- They will also need two to three servings of carbohydrate each day – bread, rice, pasta and potatoes are good, inexpensive sources.

Vegan Diets

If you are planning to wean your child on to a vegan diet, it is essential to consult a GP, dietitian or nutritionist first. All foods that are animal in origin are restricted by a vegan diet. This means that vitamins D and B, complete proteins, calcium, iron and all of the other nutrients your child needs can be difficult to provide.

Chubby Babies

Don't worry – as they begin to crawl and walk, your child should begin to lose any excess weight. At this age, it's common for most babies to be on the chubby side.

Top Tip

Try to have some food along with your child, even if you're not eating a meal. They're more likely to tuck in happily if they have a little encouragement!

Top Tip

Don't force your child to eat something if they don't like it. Wait a few weeks, then try giving it to them again. It's more than likely that they'll be happy to give it another go.

Can Babies be Vegetarians?

It is a good idea to consult your GP, a dietitian or nutritionist for advice on how to combine protein sources to ensure your child receives all the essential amino acids they need in their diet. All the nutrients your child needs to develop and thrive can be provided by a well-balanced, varied vegetarian diet. Other sources will need to be found to provide the nutrients provided by meat and fish, however.

- Eggs and tofu, as well as pulses like lentils, chickpeas and beans are all great sources of vegetable protein. Give your child two servings of these each day, alongside a carbohydrate such as rice.

- Serve fruit and vegetables along with non-meat protein, not just as snacks – the vitamin C in them will help your child to absorb more iron.

What Do I Need in My Kitchen?

Cooking for your child won't require lots of expensive equipment. The basics will include…

- Saucepan (stainless steel);
- Mouli, smoothie-maker or hand-held blender;
- Ziploc bags;
- Small plastic spoons;
- Waterproof sheet (to protect the floor under the highchair);
- Cup or baby beaker;
- Bibs;
- Highchair;

- Small bowls;
- Ice cube trays;
- Steamer.

Six Months+: The Best First Foods

- Breast milk or formula, PLUS;
- Ready Brek, Shreddies, and other breakfast cereals that are low in salt and sugar;
- Apricots, raisins, prunes and other dried fruits;
- Pureed pork, turkey, chicken and other meats;
- Small amounts of unsweetened yoghurt (no cow's milk yet!);
- Pureed vegetables (sweet potatoes, squash);
- Fruit – apples, peaches, pears, bananas, kiwi, melon, plum.
- Porridge.

Foods to Avoid at Six Months:

- Salt (babies shouldn't have too much salt as it's bad for their kidneys);
- Sugar;
- Nuts (your child can choke and may have an allergic reaction);
- "Low-fat" foods (babies and young children need the calories and vitamins they can get from a healthy amount of fat);
- Citrus fruits and berries;
- Honey (until one year);
- Butter and oil.

Nine to 12 Months: The Best First Foods

- Porridge (use unsweetened oats);
- Sandwiches (use soft bread and cut off the crusts);
- Baked potato (remove the skin);
- Eggs;
- Oily fish;
- Pasta;
- Yoghurt.

Foods to Avoid at Nine to 12 Months

- Added sugar and salt;
- Some types of fish (swordfish, tuna and shark may contain traces of mercury);
- Shellfish (until five years);
- Honey (this can contain bacteria that may damage your child's intestines).

Summing Up

- Until they are six months old, babies should be given breast milk or formula exclusively.

- Weaning on to baby rice and puréed fruits and vegetables can begin at six months old.

- You can make the texture of purées chunkier and introduce protein between seven and nine months.

- Your child can have three meals plus snacks per day from nine months onwards, at which point your child can eat the same foods as the rest of the family, minus the sugar and salt.

- Food allergies can be a risk for some children.

- Care needs to be taken with vegetarian and vegan diets to ensure your child receives sufficient nutrients.

- Dairy foods, protein, fruit, vegetables and carbohydrates are all necessary to make up a balanced diet for your child.

4

The First Five Years

et the basics right and your child can build a healthy lifestyle around what you have taught them simply by serving up quick, tasty and healthy dinners. Of course, making good food choices is more likely to happen when eating is associated with fun, rather than stress or pressure, which is why in this chapter you'll find ideas for encouraging your child to eat a great range of healthy meals, without using food as either punishment or reward. And although it's not always easy for working parents or carers to fit in a job, grocery shopping, childcare and all the other demands on your time, it should be possible to serve up home-cooked food at least part of the week.

Even as they develop their own tastes and seek out different recipes and new flavours to try, the memory of childhood meals will inform your child's food choices as an adult. That might be difficult to imagine when they're at the stage where they'll eat nothing but a bowl of cereal or play with their peas for what feels like hours, though! Delicious family meals don't require you to be an amateur chef or spend extortionate amounts on ingredients. Even one home-cooked meal a week is better than nothing (though more than this would be great!) – you could even sit down with your family and decide which meal you should prioritise eating together, no matter how busy you are, whether that's breakfast, lunch or dinner.

For parents of children aged up to five, this chapter hopes to provide information on the pitfalls of sugar, the wonders of superfoods and some common-sense advice about balancing treats.

Finding Your Family's Healthy Balance

Don't let providing good meals turn into another pressure in an already full life. And the occasional biscuit or cake can add a touch of sweetness to the day. Every family needs to find a balance of convenience and health that works for them when it comes to food. This will be affected by lots of stuff, including what you can afford to spend, how many people live in your house, the types of food you like to eat and the time you have to shop and cook in. As long as your child has no particular health problems, so long as you're able to provide healthy meals around 80% of the time you can be a little more flexible for the remaining 20%.

Fruit, nuts, seeds and vegetables make healthy snacks for mid morning or afternoon. A good place to start is always providing a nutritious breakfast. A nice mixture of healthy fats, proteins and vegetables should be made available at lunchtime. Later, vegetables, homemade soup, rice or pasta with a little protein can be served for dinner, which should be nice and early so your child has time to digest before bedtime. Make sure you're making use of seasonal fruits and vegetables.

Kids' Superfoods

Your kitchen can act as a natural medicine cabinet to keep your child as healthy as possible and aid their recovery when they do feel poorly. Young children tend to come down with a lot of stomach upsets, infections and colds, because they're pretty much a blank canvas for bugs. You can help your child to be more resistant to illness by providing them with a range of fresh, natural foods that will provide a broad spectrum of essential nutrients. Whether they're feeling on top of the world or under the weather, you can use the list below to pack your larder with foods naturally full of vitamins that will boost your child's natural immunity, slow-releasing energy to keep them going and antioxidants to fight cell damage.

How Much Fish?

Everyone should be eating at least two 140g portions of fish each week, one of which should be oily, according to government guidelines. It's important to follow guidelines for your child, however, because pollutants may be absorbed by fish when they're alive. (Source: "Fish and Shellfish" NHS, https://**www.nhs.uk/live-well/eat-well/fish-and-shellfish-nutrition**, accessed 13 November 2018.)

- We're advised not to eat any more than four portions (per week) of oily fish.

- As they contain more mercury than other fish, children, pregnant women and women who are trying to get pregnant should not eat swordfish, shark or marlin.

- Reduce your child's risk of getting food poisoning by avoiding giving them raw shellfish.

- Tinned tuna counts as white fish, as the oils are lost in the canning process.

- Boys under the age of 16 can have up to four portions of oily fish and unlimited white fish.

Fruit

Citrus Fruits

Citrus fruits are high in vitamin C, which helps your child's immune system to protect against colds, bugs and viruses. Your child's wellbeing will also be supercharged by fibre, pectin, flavonoids, phytochemicals and folic acid, all of which can be found in citrus fruits like oranges, grapefruit and lemons.

Berries

Keep berries in the fridge to maintain their nutrient content. These are some of the most popular superfoods for kids and adults alike. You can find loads of important antioxidants, potassium, calcium, vitamin C and bioflavinoids in berries like blackberries, redcurrants, blackcurrants, strawberries, cherries and blueberries.

'Always wash fresh and dried fruit well to remove any traces of dirt and pesticides.'

Apricots

Dried and fresh apricots are very popular with children thanks to their sweet taste. They are also rich sources of phytochemicals, which are good for skin health. They protect the body from recurrent infections and colds, as they're full of vitamin C. Some children may experience allergic reactions to dried apricots and other fruits preserved in sulphur dioxide, so make sure you choose a brand without this chemical (it will be marked on the label).

Apples

Wash them well and, if possible, do not peel them before serving to your child. Loads of good nutrients – such as fibre, antioxidants and vitamin C to help boost the immune system – can be found in apples, which are already popular with children thanks to their natural sweetness. They can prevent constipation in children thanks to their fibre content, while their pectin will stimulate the bacteria in your child's gut.

Grapes

If you want an alternative to chocolate and confectionary, grapes and raisins make lovely sweet snacks. Raisings (like all dried fruit) are high in sugar, so only a small handful should be given as a treat or when your child needs a burst of energy. Whichever you choose, grapes and raisins are both high in fibre and vitamins.

Bananas

Choose ripe bananas for children, as they are more easily digested. Kids love bananas, they contain heaps of tryptophan, beta carotene, fibre, vitamins C and B6 and potassium. While bananas are great when a quick burst of energy is needed (just think of all the tennis players who eat them at Wimbledon), the tryptophan they contain is also relaxing and helps to aid sleep.

Kiwi Fruits

Kiwi fruits are packed with vitamin C, potassium and fibre. Cut open and served in an eggcup with a spoon to scoop out the flesh, kiwi fruits will make a fun and tasty snack for your children.

Nuts and Allergy

Even if there is no known risk, watch carefully for signs of a reaction the first time your child has nuts; this is likely to come on within minutes of eating them and no more than four hours afterwards. If there is any family history of allergies, nuts should be avoided while your child is below the age of five.

If your child is having a mild allergic reaction to nuts, they may show symptoms such as…

- Strange sensations on the mouth and lips;
- Feeling poorly;
- Pains in the abdomen;
- Tightening of the throat;
- A rash, similar to nettle rash;
- Swelling of the face.

A more serious reaction will include symptoms like…

- Respiratory difficulties;
- Dizziness or feeling faint;
- Fast heart rate.

Seeds and Nuts

Serve nuts either chopped or ground to avoid any risk of choking, until your little one is five. Packed with nutrients to help boost your child's immunity, nut butters, nuts and seeds are a great energy-boosting food.

Linseeds (Flaxseeds)

Grind them over breakfast cereals or put a few drops of flaxseed oil into smoothies or salad dressings but do not use for cooking. Omega 3 essential fatty acids can be found in these seeds.

Sunflower Seeds

They are a good source of essential fatty acids, boosting brain function. Supercharge your child's breakfast by grinding these wonderful seeds over breakfast cereal, yoghurt or muesli.

Almonds

Magnesium, which helps children to relax, can be found in this nutritious nut, and so can essential fatty acids, which are good for the heart.

Walnuts

They're great for boosting immunity. Omega 3 essential fatty acids, protein, potassium, magnesium and vitamins B6 and E can all be found in walnuts.

Sesame Seeds

If your child is sensitive to dairy products, sesame seeds would make a great addition to their diet as they are rich in calcium. They also contain many other nutrients, including antioxidant vitamin E.

Pumpkin Seeds

Give your child pumpkin seeds from an early age to help support the immune system – they have some of the highest zinc levels of all the seeds. Omega 6 and omega 9 essential fatty acids, protein, potassium and magnesium can also be found in pumpkin seeds.

Veggies Four Ways with Vegetables

Remember to wash vegetables well before cooking and eating, peeling and removing seeds where necessary to minimise the risk of choking. You can find the method of preparing vegetables that suits your child best, thanks to their wonderful ability to be used and prepared in different ways. You might like to serve up your vegetables in one of these ways…

- Fresh – Wands of celery, strips of bell pepper and cucumber, whole mange tout and mini corn, tiny cherry tomatoes and grated carrot can all be eaten raw. Whether they're seeing how many different-colour crudités they can fill their plate with, figuring out the best vegetable for dipping in hummus or eating celery filled with soft cheese, kids will love the opportunity to play with their food. Raw vegetables have the ability to aid digestion and provide energy – their natural enzymes haven't been killed off by cooking, so the body can use them for a wide range of functions.

- Dry-Roasted – If you want a beautiful-looking plateful of veggies, roasting is a great way to intensify natural flavours and deepen colours. It's a great way to cook sweet or starchy vegetables. Olive oil and hemp oil are good options, but there are loads of different cooking oils out there. If your child doesn't love them at first, try again with a different oil.

- Soups and juices – While you wait for your child to fall in love with broccoli, you can try these tricks to increase their vegetable intake: make vegetable soup (great served with a crouton of bread and toasted cheese); purée the vegetables and use them as a sauce with rice or a small type of pasta; disguise loathed vegetables with those your child does like, such as stirring puréed peppers or carrots into a favourite tomato sauce; and make delicious juices that introduce them to the taste of vegetables before they try them again whole (you can dilute vegetable juices with water or combine with fruit juices to make them more palatable).

- Steamed – Lightly steaming vegetables makes them easy and tasty to eat, while preserving as many of their nutrients as possible (these can leach into the cooking water if you boil them). If your child prefers, drizzle steamed vegetables with extra virgin olive oil and lemon.

Sweet Potatoes

Sweet potatoes are packed with vitamin C, calcium, magnesium and beta carotene. Sweet potato even promotes strong teeth and healthy gums in children. Loads of kids love the sweet flavour of this humble potato. It can be mashed, baked or added into vegetable soups. They help the body's chemistry to maintain a healthy nervous system thanks to their high calcium and magnesium content.

Garlic, Onion and Leeks

Antibacterial, antiseptic and antiviral properties are held by members of this family of vegetables. They are also high in vitamin C and the mineral selenium, which plays an important role in protecting against cancer and heavy metal toxicity. For a potent antibiotic, try chowing down on some food rich in garlic. Garlic's potential health benefits seem to come from the compound allicin, which is released only when the garlic is chopped or crushed.

Carrots

Carrots are a great food to boost immunity and liver function. Protecting against viruses and infections, this sweet, colourful vegetable is packed with beta carotene, which the body converts into vitamin A. Children with skin conditions such as eczema will also benefit from beta carotene's complexion-friendly qualities.

Cabbage, Brussels Sprouts, Cauliflower and Broccoli

They do have a strong taste, which some children find off putting, but try mixing in small amounts with other vegetables until your child is used to the flavour. These all belong to a family called brassicas, which contain important nutrients like folic acid, vitamin K, beta carotene and iron as well as being rich in fibre.

Tomatoes

As well as immunity-boosting vitamin C, they contain lycopene, a powerful antioxidant that helps to prevent cell damage. Whether they're served in a mini salad with dinner or used as a snack between meals, many children love tomatoes. Too many tomatoes may reduce absorption of calcium, though, so don't go too crazy! If you can, it's also a good idea to cut back on ketchup.

Are You a Fun Guy?

Zinc is important, as a lack is linked to poor resistance to infections, skin conditions such as eczema and sleeplessness in young children. Mushrooms provide a great source of zinc, B vitamins, iron, folic acid, protein and other vital nutrients.

String Beans

They are rich in vitamins A and C, and are a good food for helping skin disorders. Also known as green beans, children tend to love these vegetables.

Beans and Pulses

See chapter 2 on what foods to eat with pulses and beans to ensure your child gets the right protein balance. These are a great choice – as well as protein, legumes contain both soluble and insoluble fibres to keep the intestinal tract healthy, and they provide a good source of vitamins, minerals such as zinc and iron, and isoflavones. Beans and pulses are beloved by many children, who find them easier to digest or chew than meat and similar dishes. If you store them in a dry, cool place in an airtight container, beans will make a great store cupboard food as the dried varieties can keep for up to a year.

Soya

Calcium, protein, thiamine, iron and fibre are all packed into the humble soya bean.

Chickpeas

Chickpeas are rich in calcium, magnesium, zinc, potassium, beta carotene and folic acids. They're great puréed into homemade hummus or stirred into stews and salads.

Lentils and Dals

Young children often prefer the mild orange lentils, but green and brown lentils are excellent cooked in stews and casseroles. Loads of vital nutrients like folic acid, vegetable proteins, iron, magnesium, zinc, calcium and some B vitamins are all packed into lentils. To increase your child's absorption of iron, give your child foods rich in vitamin C to eat alongside the lentils.

Garden Peas

High in thiamin (vitamin B1), vitamin C and niacin. Peas strengthen digestion and improve constipation. Kids love them for their bright green colour and sweet taste, and the peas love them right back.

Taste the Rainbow

Eating by colours is a great way of helping you to plan menus. It also fires your child's imagination about what they are eating. Because different colours are associated with certain health benefits, it's a good idea to serve meals that combine as many colours as possible. This will help us to maximise the range of nutrients our child has in one sitting.

A quick way of checking that the meal has a good balance of vitamins, minerals, proteins, carbohydrates and fats is to imagine the colour of your lunch, supper or breakfast.

Pink	Seafood and rhubarb.
Red	Berries, watermelon, tomatoes and peppers.
Orange	Apricots, oranges, papaya, swede and carrots.
Yellow	Sweet corn, butternut squash, lemon and egg yolk.
Green	Vegetables and fruits.
Blue	Berries.
White	Chicken, milk, turkey and fish.
Brown	Pulses, nuts and grains.

What's Wrong with Sugar?

Tempting your child into healthy, delicious foods is often made easier by the sweet tooth most children are born with, which helps them to enjoy the natural sugars in sweet potatoes, melons, mangoes, sweet peppers, carrots and parsnips. Sadly, though, the sugar they're exposed to won't always be this healthy, natural sugar. Yoghurts, sweets, chocolate and cakes are all packed with sugar, which can lead to poor behaviour and health problems if your child eats them in excess. It's best to limit the number of sweet foods your child eats from an early age.

The problem isn't even limited to sweet treats. Blood sugar is pushed high above normal levels by refined foods, which are low in fibre and high in simple carbohydrates that are converted rapidly by the body into glucose. Unhealthy eating habits can develop in later life if you cheer up, quieten or reward your child with sweets as it sets up a connection between sugar and "being good" or "feeling better". The following problems may also develop as a result of excess sugar…

- Changes in mood – Your child may begin to feel tired, grumpy, depressed, hyperactive or moody if they have too much sugar. Refined foods are depleted of B vitamins, and this is often a major cause of these mood changes. Behavioural changes like anxiety and depressions can be aggravated or caused by a deficiency in B vitamins (especially B1).

- Poor dental health – An acidic environment may be created when sugar increases the bacteria in your child's mouth. The teeth will become more prone to decay as this acid begins to attack their enamel.

- Weight gain – Obesity can be dealt with satisfactorily with good nutrition, and monitoring sugar levels is a big part of that (though it should be noted that obesity is also tied with genetics).

- Problems in the GI tract – The balance of the gut can be disturbed by excess sugar.

- Weakened immune system – too much sugar has been associated with a reduction in the amount of minerals available to the body to help fight disease.

- Long-term health problems – When sugar and refined foods are eaten in excess, the sugar contained in them disturbs the metabolism of glucose in the body, contributing to diabetes, hypoglycaemia (low blood sugar), high blood pressure and heart problems. The rise in child diabetes has been linked with high sugar intake.

- Cravings – The way that the body processes excess sugar can actually lead to a desire for more, ultimately putting your child's organs under strain as they try to cope with the sharp highs and lows in blood sugar levels.

Eating Sugar Creates a Cycle

Your child's energy to climb trees, dance and run about in the playground comes from their ability to convert any carbohydrates they consume into an energy-packed sugar called glucose. According to the body's needs, blood glucose levels are increased and decreased by two hormones produced in the pancreas – insulin and glucagon. Our blood sugar level is pushed well above its level when we eat a meal that contains sugar or refined products (simple carbohydrates) which the body can digest and absorb very quickly. The spike in sugar causes the pancreas to release the hormone insulin, which can then break down the glucose. We then begin to crave more sugary foods because this sudden reduction in blood sugar has caused our bodies to feel a drop in energy. This is the beginning of a negative and unhealthy cycle.

Breaking the Cycle

If you prevent a spike in their blood sugar and the subsequent release of insulin, you'll stop the sudden dramatic fall in glucose that leads to a dip in energy and the craving for more sugar. Slowing down the production of glucose is the key to balancing the sugar level in your child's body. Eating foods that provide a steady release of energy is the best way to do this. Here are some quick tips:

- Instead of refined versions that release sugar into the body too quickly, give your child complex carbohydrates like wholemeal bread and rice.

- Help your child's food to release glucose more slowly by pairing carbohydrates with protein.

- Be careful when you're choosing your sweet treats. Pick cereals that are sweetened with raisins and other dried fruits rather than ones that are coated in sugar. While these will still have plenty of sugar in them, they'll also be rich in nutrients and fibre.

- Get baking – Making your own pastries, cakes and biscuits is fun for you and your child. Adapt recipes so that you use wholemeal flour (try swapping white flour for wholemeal, or use a mix of 50:50 white flour and wholemeal) and reduced sugar – they'll still taste delicious.

- Read labels carefully – Juices that claim "no added sugar" may be rich in fructose, the natural fruit sugar, which has the same effect on dental decay as sugar. If you can, make your own fruit juices and dilute them with water. Otherwise, add water to bought fresh juices.

- Combine simple carbohydrates with fibre, which will help to slow down digestion and the release of sugar.

Summing Up

- Even when your child grows up, their food choices will be influenced by the meals you served them as a child.

- Nut allergies are serious – always keep an eye out for potential symptoms.

- Your child's health and behaviour can be negatively influenced by a diet high in sugar.

- Every family should find its own healthy food balance.

- Meals that contain foods of lots of different colours will contain a broad range of nutrients.

- Eating a broad range of natural foods will help to boost your child's immunity to illness and help them to recover more quickly.

5

Children Aged Six to 10

This is the perfect age to start your child's exploration of the kitchen (supervised by you, of course). This chapter will look at how to encourage your child to eat a wide range of foods, because even a child who loves to cook may need a little extra encouragement to swallow their greens sometimes. Turning basic foodstuffs into meals is sort of like magic, and when your child gets involved you are letting them become part of the show. They can't wait to knead the dough for homemade pizza or sieve flour for biscuits.

Allowing your little ones to discover the wonder of ingredients can be a spellbinding lesson. You can help your child to grow up healthy and strong while they learn how to stir, measure and chop, by teaching them how each food works in the body. We'll provide some ideas for healthy meals and snacks for six to 10 year olds, as well as tackling the challenging subject of the school lunch box. The information here on essential vitamins and brain-boosting foods will help you to give your child a nutritional foundation for effective learning and power them through sports days, plays and after-school activities.

These are the years when school becomes more demanding, and can come as a bit of a shock compared to the play-based learning of reception classes.

Quick Tip

Keep knives and other sharp objects far from reach and make sure they don't go near the oven or hob. It's best to use only a few utensils at a time when you cook with your child, so that you can explain the uses for each one: Why are you using a washable chopping board to prepare meat? Why does a colander have so many holes?

'Cooking with children is messy, but it's worth it to watch how much they enjoy eating food they have prepared themselves.'

Healthy Lunchboxes

Wholegrain sliced or pitta bread is the best option, but it's fine to give children white bread once or twice a week – it's all about balance. Try to send your child to school with some highly nutritious sandwiches. Along with fruit and vegetable snacks like baby carrots, an easy-peel orange, pepper slices, cherry tomatoes or celery sticks, there's nothing wrong with popping in a biscuit as a treat.

If you are at home, give your child a small apple, pear, banana, tangerine, or a few dates or dried apricots. As a mid-morning snack, lots of schools now provide their pupils with fruit. When you're making dinner on a school night, try preparing some extra salad or vegetables to save time when preparing packed lunches.

Nutritious & Simple Lunchbox Fillers

Fromage Frais, Alfalfa and Tomatoes

Spread fromage frais on two slices of granary bread, and top with sliced tomato and washed alfalfa sprouts (similar to cress).

Mozzarella or Egg in a Bagel with Tomatoes and Avocado

Slice the bagel open and fill it with sliced mozzarella (or sliced, hard-boiled egg). Drizzle with a little olive oil. Lay out sliced avocado and tomatoes on top. Include a handful of low-salt crisps as a side.

Hummus and Pitta Bread

Packed with vitamins to keep your child's energy going, hummus is made from tahini paste and chickpeas. Sliced tomatoes make a great side. Plus, a homemade blueberry muffin.

Cucumber with Cottage Cheese

Wash the cucumber, and chop it into a variety of sticks and slices. Spread whole wheat bread with cottage cheese, laying cucumber slices on top. Pack this in a lunchbox alongside two chocolate fingers, some baby carrots and cucumber sticks.

Pitta Bread with Eggs and Vegetables

If you've had steamed vegetables like broccoli or carrots for dinner, set some aside to mix with scrambled eggs in a pitta. Plus, a ripe pear.

Watercress, Onion and Tuna

Chop a small onion and two cherry tomatoes, add a tin of tuna and mix well. Prepare this sandwich with sliced rye bread. Spread the bread with the tuna mixture, and lay washed, chopped watercress on top.

The First Cooking Lesson

Teaching your child about how food is prepared is incredibly important, and it's never too early to get started. On your own weekly shop, your child can help to choose fresh fruits and vegetables and talk about what meals you will make with them. A toddler can help to stir a cake mixture, a three or four year old can help to roll out pastry, and a child of five or six can begin to measure out ingredients and even chop up vegetables, under your watchful eye. So long as they're kept out of harm's way, a baby can be brought into the kitchen in their highchair so that they can watch you make dinner. Pretend to cook or buy groceries outside of the kitchen by playing with toy foodstuffs with your child.

Younger children can use a plastic knife in the kitchen and help by cutting the softer foods. This 'game' also teaches them the importance of food hygiene, as you teach them to wash their hands before they start and at the end of cooking, and make sure the surfaces and equipment are clean. Kids love slicing up celery, peppers and cucumber to make their own side salad. This is a great tip for any parent who wants their child to eat more vegetables: yes, they'll make a mess, but it'll be worth it when you see how much they enjoy eating the food they've prepared.

Angela's Case Study: The Boy who Didn't Like Vegetables

At six years old, Frank's son George would only eat the vegetables that tasted the sweetest – potatoes, carrots and sweetcorn. I explained to Frank that most young children prefer sweet-tasting vegetables but that they develop a liking for stronger flavours as they mature. Frank was desperate to improve his son's diet by expanding his menu to include more minerals, flavours and colours.

When they refuse to try anything new, it's not uncommon for young children like George to become 'stuck' in their food choices. At the end of the day, struggling with certain foods or flavours is normal for many of us, not just children. These blocks aren't permanent, though, and there are strategies that can help a child to get over them.

The next time they went shopping they were to pick colourful vegetables so that they could 'cook a rainbow' – carrots, marrow, spinach, sweet potatoes, aubergines, red peppers, cauliflower… I also asked Frank and George to choose some easy-to-grow vegetables, such as tomatoes, salad leaves and peas, and to plant some seeds or plants in pots or in the garden, so that George could have the pleasure of eating the food he had grown himself. I advised Frank to start preparing alternative vegetables just in case, so that when George refused a vegetable he could take it away and replace it without a fuss.

He could offer George the rejected vegetable the next day, this time presented on a different plate and cooked in a different way. He should also make sure that George was hungry when he sat down to eat by cutting down on sugary snacks between meals that would simply reinforce his taste for sweetness and decrease his appetite. He should keep trying different ways of preparing and presenting the vegetables until he found something that worked. Involving George in choosing the vegetables they were to eat was another potential solution.

If Frank and George worked together to chop and cook the vegetables and present them in a rainbow pattern, George could be encouraged to eat vegetables of each colour so he could get all of the nutrients available.

My final piece of advice was for Frank to treat mealtimes as normally as possible, without appearing tense every time George sat down for dinner.

At first, George's case was a tricky one. Three weeks after our consultation, Frank called me to say he'd tried all of my suggestions but that it hadn't helped. I asked him to cook minestrone soup, whiz it in the blender, then add some small cooked pasta shapes, rice, or roasted bread cut into tiny pieces. I asked him to try more new ways to include vegetables in George's diet, and to persist with my methods. Brussels sprouts with a little butter and grated almonds was one recipe that might work, I suggested, or an omelette with lots of asparagus or green beans, pasta with broccoli or zucchine ripiene (stuffed courgettes). With time, George learned to eat mixed salad and even seemed to like his vegetables. Frank's patience had paid off, and he was very relieved.

Let Your Brain Breathe

Fresh fruit and vegetables are vital brain-boosting ingredients that you need to include in your child's diet. Berries, such as blueberries, are a great addition to your child's diet. They help to maintain a good supply of oxygen to the brain cells, as they're rich in the powerful antioxidants vitamins C and E. Vitamin B12 helps to maintain the fatty myelin sheath that protects nerve tissue, while vitamin C is needed to help form the brain's neurotransmitters. If your child has cereal or yoghurt for breakfast, try sprinkling a handful of berries over the top for added nutrition and flavour.

Angela's Case Study: A Picky Eater

Suffering from frequent tummy aches and colds, Dean was brought to see me when he was seven years old. I spoke to his father, Evan, about his diet, and it became clear that Dean's diet was overloaded with dairy products and milk, and that he was eating far too many fatty and sugary snacks. Dean's repetitive diet was lacking in the nutrients found in good fats, vegetables and fruit. Evan said that he had tried everything possible to make him eat a larger variety, but had been unsuccessful. Dean was simply an incredibly picky eater.

The continual intake of sugary foods impoverished the friendly bacteria in his gut, causing tummy problems. Dairy products can increase the formation of excessive mucus, and the large quantity he ate was not helping his frequent colds. Dean told me that he wanted to be an astronaut when he grew up, and I encouraged him to eat more healthily to feed his brain and body, so that he would be fit and strong enough to go for his goal. I explained to Dean that our body is like a car, with the brain as its motor.

His immune system had become weakened as a result of his diet. So as not to frighten him with a drastic change to his diet, I gave him a list of some products he could still eat instead of cutting out all dairy. I explained to Dean and Evan that complex carbohydrates like whole grains were far more nutritious than refined carbohydrates (white flour products). These white flour products were causing him to crave more sugary foods, as they caused his blood sugar level to drop too fast. Carbohydrates such as bread, pasta and rice are the petrol; protein, including meat, fish and pulses, are the building blocks that renew and repair the machinery; and fats such as olive oil and fish oils keep the machine lubricated and functioning smoothly. Good fuel is needed to power the human body, because it's a very complicated machine. If we want to make sure that every part of this machine is working well with the others, we need to be giving it minerals and vitamins from fruits and vegetables, the hidden helpers that keep it all going.

It really does help to explain to a child the way that food works in the body and that eating a balanced diet will bring them closer to achieving their dreams. Dean no longer suffered from poor health when I talked to Evan again three months later. He had become a completely different boy who snacked on fruit instead of sweet treats and always ate vegetables with his dinner.

Dealing with Picky Eaters

As parents, it can be hard to stay calm and detach as your child pushes their peas around their plate or won't swallow their roast chicken. It can be tough when your little one is reluctant to eat a certain food. Nothing can ruin a child's appetite quite like dinner table tension! When it comes to tackling what's on your plate, you're the best judge of whether your child will benefit most from fun and joking, rewards systems, gentle encouragement or something else entirely. However, the following strategies can be a good place to start:

- What you would like your child to try and what they want to eat can all be discussed before you head to the shops. Work as a team to plan your meals and menus.

- Have conversations about why certain foods are healthy or unhealthy, and where different foods come from.

- Help your child to understand that while no foods are "bad", some need to be eaten in smaller amounts if they want to feel healthy and strong.

- Children will often try previously refused foods when they see their friends enjoying them. Try having your child's friends around for dinner so they can eat together and have fun.

- Keep a healthy stock of fruit, vegetables, wholegrains, lean proteins and healthy cheeses in the kitchen and explain why you have chosen them. Simply seeing foods frequently can help them to become familiar and inspire your child to try them out.

- Have fun with the way you present food. Try making faces on the plate with it (try a slice of toast with black olives for eyes, yellow pepper slices for eyebrows, cherry tomatoes for a nose and lips, and salad leaves for hair – and that smiling food friend will soon be in your child's stomach.

- Use fun images to get your child excited about eating. Why not say that all the healthy foods are invited to a party in their tummy – couldn't they eat their carrots so they could join the broccoli for some fun?

- Involve your child in preparing and cooking meals when you can.

As long as they are eating a wide range of other foods, an occasional 'no' shouldn't leave a nutritional gap in their diet. You will need to let your child lead the way in some cases. Some children will happily eat mince but find it difficult to swallow roast beef for example. Over time, you'll learn to tell the difference between your child inventing foods to dislike, and your child genuinely disliking or struggling with a certain type of food. If your child has had a bad experience with a certain food (such as burning their tongue because a mouthful was too hot, or coincidentally getting sick after eating it), never push them to eat it. In their own time, they will be ready to try this food again.

'Explaining that the body is like a motor and that it needs fuel and the right parts to make it run, will encourage your child to eat.'

Quick Tip

Your child can snack on healthy seeds to keep their body and brain going throughout the day. Sardines on wholegrain toast or a sandwich made with tuna on whole wheat bread is a great lunch option for your child.

The Protein-Carbohydrate Partnership

Research shows that children who eat a breakfast containing equivalent amounts of complex carbohydrates and protein learn and perform better than those who eat either a high-protein or a high-carbohydrate breakfast. Complex carbohydrates help to keep sugar levels balanced and also help to carry amino acids from proteins into the brain. It is important to give the right carbohydrates and to team them with protein in order to keep blood sugar levels in balance.

Brain cells will die if they have to go without their two favourite nutrients – oxygen and glucose – for even a few seconds. They need a continuous supply. Both learning and behaviour can suffer when blood sugar levels fluctuate, as the brain's ability to function becomes impaired. Providing a balance of energy and the building blocks of brain chemicals to help them study, lunches and breakfasts containing protein and complex carbohydrates are the ideal way to stimulate your child's brain and set them up for the day. Unsweetened natural yoghurt with fresh fruit, low-sugar cereals like Oatibix and Bran Flakes and porridge are all good breakfast options.

'The brain is part of the body and needs the same nourishing care.'

Quick Tip

Now that they're governed by strict nutritional guidelines, parents no longer need to discount school meals as a healthy option. Try to encourage your child to select at least one portion each of vegetables and fruit; a food containing protein like fish, nuts or chicken; and a carbohydrate like rice, bread or potatoes.

The Magic of Brain Food

We'll often talk about foods that help to give the best resistance to diseases, keep the bones strong, joints supple and heart healthy when we discuss good nutrition for children and adults alike. We tend to focus on the body. But if we want to function healthily, we need to feed our brains with antioxidant-rich fruits and vegetables, fats to help the brain send messages all around the body, and glucose to give the brain energy to run. The same nourishing care should be given to the brain as to the rest of our body.

Your child needs all of this nourishing care in the years between six and ten. At school, they'll be expected to take in a vast amount of information over these few short years. Governing all of this is the brain, which works like a computer to control your child's body, store memories, control moods and translate the environment around them. Your child is learning how to process the amazing but complicated feelings that come with friendship, playing, responsibility and families, and is trying to work out their place in the world.

Fats: Food for Thought?

Using a massive 60% of all the energy from the food they eat, your child's brain will have tripled in size before their first birthday. This amazing organ is made mainly of fat and to keep it working well your child needs essential fatty acids – 'essential' because the body can't make them itself. Feeding the brain with the best food will remain vitally important throughout their childhood, although the organ's rate of growth slows down after the first 12 months. You can read more about essential fatty acids and the foods that contain them in Chapter 2.

Avoid foods that list 'hydrogenated' or 'partially hydrogenated' fats on the food label, as they interfere with nerve function. Because they have a negative impact on the brain and on the health in general, your child should have limited access to fats from processed or fried foods. They can cause less blood to reach the brain as they are dense and can pack blood vessels. They'll also reduce your child's appetite for healthy foods that are naturally high in the essential fatty acids omega 3 and 6, as they will have filled up on chips, buns, biscuits and pastries.

How Does Good Behaviour Tie In with Food?

Low blood sugar and meals that are low in nutrients can result in all sorts of negative behaviours like restlessness, moodiness, irritability, tiredness and poor concentration. That's why giving your child a good breakfast to start the day and providing them with a healthy school lunch is so important. Your child will find it difficult to interact positively with teachers and fellow pupils, and to learn and enjoy their time at school, if they aren't eating right.

- 'Eating breakfast may improve children's problem solving abilities, their memory, concentration levels, visual perception and thinking,' according to Lisa Miles, senior nutritionist at the British Nutrition Foundation. (Source: Breakfast and Behaviour, **www.teachers.tv**.)

- 'Having a healthy, balanced diet improves brain capacity, maximizes cognitive capabilities, and improves academic performance in school age children.' (Source: Nutrition and Academic Performance in School-Age Children: The Relation to Obesity and Food Insufficiency, Journal of Nutrition & Food Sciences, 2013.)

Speedy Snacking

These inexpensive, delicious snacks are light enough not to spoil your child's lunch or dinner, and are much better for them than crisps and cakes. Children eat smaller portions than adults because they have small stomachs. To fuel their activities, however, they need a regular supply of energy.

- Miniature cheeses;
- Popcorn (it's nutritious and whole grain!);
- Celery with peanut butter and raisins (also known as "ants on a log");
- Warm milk and homemade biscuits;
- Rice cakes spread with hummus and served with dried apricots;
- Yoghurt (a good source of protein and calcium).

Summing Up

- Teach your child about the wonder of foods when they're very young. Encourage them to cook with you and help you choose ingredients.

- Accept the occasional 'no', and figure out different ways to serve food to encourage your child to eat a wider range of foods.

- School lunches and snacks don't have to be difficult or expensive to prepare. They can provide essential nutrients for your growing child.

- Your child needs a balanced intake of carbohydrates and proteins, good fats, vitamins and minerals, to help brain development and functioning.

- Explain that there are no bad foods, just some we need to eat more than others.

6

11, 12 and Teenage Years

A healthy diet can help your child cope with other challenges associated with the teenage years, such as skin problems, exam stress, emotional wellbeing and weight concerns. As they reach adolescence, the nutritional needs of your child will change. Lean protein, good fats, complex carbohydrates and an adequate intake of vitamins and minerals should be part of their diet now. They will require specific nutrients to support their hormonal development, as well as a larger amount of calories to fuel their body's increased needs.

During puberty, they'll need extra zinc to support hormonal changes, and calcium and iron to help their body to develop fully. TV, magazines and the internet will have a big influence on how they believe they should look and what they should eat. Frustratingly, this may also be the moment they pick to start taking control of their own meals as a way of testing their new independence, and the choices they make won't always be the most nutritional options. For example, rather than the healthy lunchbox you have prepared, peer pressure might see them joining their friends for fast food at lunchtime. It's also common for teenagers to go on diets, or skip meals altogether.

Hormone Helpers

Hormones make it possible for your child to transition from childhood to early adulthood during the adolescent years. This generally involves a rapid emotional and physical growth spurt, which can run a lot smoother if you add the nutrients below to their balanced diet. Poor nutrition at this stage can affect growth and delay sexual development. For boys, this spurt usually happens between the ages of 12 and 15, and for girls it's generally 10 to 13.

'Calcium, iron and zinc are super-nutrients for every teenager.'

- An increase in muscle mass and body size (especially in boys) requires macronutrients to use as fuel. We've discussed these in greater detail in Chapter Two.

- Anaemia can be prevented by upping your teen's iron intake. If your child has their period, this will be especially important.

- Seaweed, iodised salt and seafood are all great sources of iodine, which is needed to support the thyroid.

- Newly synthesised cells benefit greatly from vitamins A, C and E. The release of some hormones is controlled by the endocrine system, which also benefits from a diet high in vitamin C.

- Zinc is essential for protein synthesis and the activity of several enzymes.

- Calcium and vitamin D have an impact on hormone secretion, and help to increase the density and growth of bones. Vitamin D, as well as being obtained from foods such as butter, margarine, oily fish and fortified cereals, is produced in the body during exposure to sunlight.

- Vitamin B for energy metabolism.

Caring through Food

Parents, carers and schools play an essential supportive role for adolescents, and offering a diet that meets their individual needs is another form of guidance and protection. Eating and sharing food with your teenager can be a vital means of support and communication during adolescence, though they may not want you to serve a healthy casserole when their friends come for dinner and won't always have time to sit down with you for lunch on busy weekends. Healthy snacks can help fuel homework and calm raging emotions, a hearty weekend breakfast can provide the perfect opportunity for a catchup, and working together to prepare oven-baked chips and homemade pizzas is a healthier, more sociable alternative to ordering a takeaway.

Foods for Clear Skin

The skin is the largest organ of the body and what we eat can directly affect its health. From pimples and blackheads to acne, skin problems are a major issue for many teenagers. A poor diet combined with a surge of hormones during puberty that stimulates oil-producing glands are the main culprits here. Try getting your teenager to eat these skin-healthy foods, rather than scarring themselves by squeezing spots or spending all their pocket money on skin-cleansing products.

- Oily fish – salmon, sardines and mackerel contain omega 3 fatty acids that help to protect the skin from damage. Their high protein content promotes the production of complexion-boosting collagen.

- Almonds and sunflower seeds – these provide the skin with great sun protection. They're loaded with vitamin E, an antioxidant which protects the skin from free radicals, which are damaging agents that can come from things like pollution and UV rays.

- Oysters, fortified cereal, pork, poultry and lean meat – these foods can all give the skin a youthful glow. They're full of iron and zinc, which are vital to healthy, functioning skin.

- Wholegrain bread, rice and pasta – these complex carbohydrates will satisfy your teenager's appetite, making them less likely to reach for skin-damaging sugary snacks. The good fibre they contain will also help the elimination of toxins from the body – another way to promote beautiful skin.

- Orange fruits and vegetables – apricots, pomegranates, papaya and mango are rich in vitamin A and beta carotene, which aid skin health. Carrots have been shown to have a beneficial effect on psoriasis and eczema.

- Citrus fruits, broccoli, red peppers and strawberries – the foods give the skin a smooth structure. They're full of vitamin C, which is vital for the production of collagen, the skin's support structure.

'A diet can restrict an adolescent's supply of nutrients just when they need them most. It's best to look at what they eat, not how much.'

Eating Disorders

If you have any concerns about your teenager's eating habits and attitudes to food, consult your GP or a specialist in eating disorders. Young people between the ages of 12 and 25 are most likely to be affected by eating disorders, and the problem affects girls more than boys – the National Institute of Health and Clinical Excellence estimates around 11% of those affected by an eating disorder are male (Source: **www.beateatingdisorders.org.uk**, accessed 25 November 2018).

Bulimia (binge eating followed by purging through food restriction, vomiting, exercise or taking laxatives in order not to gain weight) and anorexia (restriction of food) are just two of the eating disorders that leading UK eating disorder charity Beat believes to affect around 1.25 million people in the UK, both diagnosed and undiagnosed. Any number of different factors and traumatic events (including abuse, divorce, low self-esteem, bullying, illness, difficult relationships with family or friends and bereavement) may combine to cause an eating disorder. Parts are also played by an individual's genetic makeup and the impact of the media.

Malnutrition can easily occur as a result of an eating disorder, a simple and dangerous effect no matter what the cause. Long-term effects of an eating disorder might include significant health problems like osteoporosis, heart, kidney and digestive problems, and infertility.

'If you suspect your teenager may have an eating disorder, consult your GP for more advice.'

Triggers for Overeating

One common temptation is to turn to "comfort foods" that are high in sugar and fat, which stimulate a feel-good emotional response in the brain and provide an instant hit of energy. The result is a diet high in calories that are stored as fat in the body. Common teenage experiences such as stress, imbalanced blood sugar and emotional upset can all cause your teen to reach for food by triggering a response in the hypothalamus in the brain. Sadly, many of the foods they're reaching for will make matters worse by being burned up quickly, creating the need to eat these foods over and over again.

What Nutrients Do Teenagers Need?

Iron

The most easily absorbed form of iron is found in meat. In order for blood to deliver oxygen to every cell in the body, iron is needed. You can also get it from dried fruits, lentils and beans, and leafy green vegetables. Your teenager may be at risk of iron deficiency if their diet doesn't contain these foods.

Calcium

A lack of calcium-rich green vegetables in the diet, as well as too many carbonated drinks that deplete calcium levels, can mean a teenager's diet is low in this important mineral. A range of body processes, such as the formation of strong teeth and bones, rely on calcium.

Zinc

Children are very vulnerable to zinc deficiency. Zinc is a trace mineral essential for bone growth, hormonal support, energy production and healthy skin. It also boosts the immune system. Hyperactivity, slow growth rate and learning problems may all come as a result of low zinc levels.

Food Tips for Parents of Adolescents

- Never forget the value of home cooking. You can help to make up for any fast foods your teen picks up when they're out and about by serving healthy meals at home. Try to avoid processed foods, as they aren't very nutritious and are full of salt, chemical additives, artificial colourings, fats and sugar. Your teenager might even enjoy cooking for the family once a week, though you mustn't pressure them to if they have homework!

- Choosing healthy foods should be easy. Don't make your teenager work to find something healthy to eat. Buy whole wheat bread instead of white, offer salads with olive oil and lemon juice instead of fattier dressings and replace sweetened cereal with sugar-free options.

- Become a role model. Your teenager's attitude to food will be greatly influenced by the choices you make. Eat your meals together, discuss likes and dislikes, and work together on meal plans.

- Teach your teenager how to read labels. Weight-conscious teenagers can opt for low-fat foods that are actually high in sugar. Show them how to decode ingredient lists so they make informed choices.

- Sort out some snacks. Teenagers can be reluctant to sit and eat a larger meal. Keep healthy snacks in the fridge, such as washed and chopped vegetables, yoghurt, bread sticks and hummus. Have a bowl of fruit ready to grab and go.

Dealing with Emotional Rollercoasters

'The fast foods and sugary snacks your child eats with friends won't have such an impact if your serve healthy meals at home.'

Rapid mental and physical growth can make early adolescence a trying time. The surge of hormones during puberty will change their body and impact on their emotions. New cognitive connections will be filling your teenager's brain. And all of this will be taking place while your teenager experiences a new pressure to conform to the expectations of parents and carers, get good grades and earn the respect of their peers.

If you add a poor diet the result can be mood swings, emotional outbursts and irritability. The body's levels of noradrenaline and adrenaline (neurotransmitters associated with motivation and energy) and serotonin (the neurotransmitter associated with sleep and good mood) and be thrown out of balance by all of these demands and changes.

Happy Meal Remedy – Turkey Burgers

Found in turkey as well as chicken, beans, eggs and tofu, tryptophan is an essential acid that can soothe the mood.

Salmon and Brown Rice – The Natural Happy Meal

A fast mood and energy boost can be experienced if your teen eats sugary and processed foods. However, they may then feel confused, grumpy, hyperactive or spaced out when their blood sugar levels crash shortly afterwards. A more lasting boost to brainpower and happiness levels can be felt if they eat whole grains and foods rich in omega 3 fats instead.

Stir-Fry Satay Chicken with Greens – The Healthy Happy Meal

B vitamins have the power to help reduce stress, support the nervous system and boost energy and learning ability. You can find them in nuts (including peanuts), whole grains and green leafy vegetables.

Surviving Exam Time

Your teenager will be dealing with a great amount of stress when exam time rolls round. If your teenager is eating foods that help to boost their energy, focus and emotional wellbeing, they're one step closer to success. Breakfast and lunch can be missed as they rush out the door to the exam hall. Quick-fix energy boosts from caffeine and sugary snacks can become very tempting during their long hours of revision. Planning a menu of exam-friendly options is one way a parent or carer can try to take the strain out of mealtimes.

- Every day, try to give your teen foods that contain zinc, iron, folic acid, calcium, B vitamins and essential fatty acids. Choose nutritious foods that will boost their health and performance, and plan all of your meals in advance.

- The immune system can be suppressed by sugary foods, so try to keep these to a minimum.

- Breakfast is needed to provide fuel for your teenager's mind and body throughout the day, so make sure they don't skip it.

- Eating too much animal protein in the same day may overload the digestive system. Try to make one meal an easily digested vegetable soup or pulses with rice.

- Buy a stock of fresh fruit and vegetables for meals and snacks.

Menu Ideas for Exam Week

Drinks

Avoid fizzy drinks and squash as they are high in sugar and artificial additives. Try to opt for diluted fresh fruit juices or filtered water.

Breakfast

- A teaspoon of wheat germ, a tablespoon of mixed seeds and a handful of blueberries, all sprinkled over porridge.

- Avocado toast, or a boiled egg with toasted soldiers.

- Plain yoghurt with blueberries or a sliced banana, and one teaspoon of mixed seeds.

'If you are extremely worried about your teenager's happiness or mental wellbeing, consult your GP or another health professional.'

Morning Snack

- Strawberries.
- Carrot sticks with hummus.
- Mixed nuts.
- Seeds.
- Yoghurt.

Lunch and Dinner

- Grilled fresh fish with carrots and cabbage.
- Organic brown rice with homemade vegetable soups (like carrot and coriander, or leek and potato).
- Mixed vegetables and steamed potatoes with white fish.
- Sweet potatoes with lean meat and green beans.
- Fish with green beans.
- Rice with cooked vegetables and chicken.
- Chicken or turkey with carrots and sweet potatoes.

Is Your Teenager Overweight?

In the UK, obesity in boys aged between five and 19 has risen from 2.4% in 1975 to 10.9% in 2016, while obesity in girls rose from 3% in 1975 to 9.4% in 2016 (Source: Childhood obesity soars worldwide, 2017, **www.nhs.uk**, accessed 25 November 2018). Many charities and government organisations are deeply concerned by the number of overweight and obese children and young people in the UK today.

But it's important to remember that adolescence is a period of rapid growth and development, and that will naturally result in increased appetite. You may be concerned about how much your teenager eats if you're their carer or guardian. During puberty, your teen needs to build up a store of energy that can fuel the many physical changes that are happening to their body. Without providing excess calories, it's necessary to provide a diet that will support this growth spurt. Physical activities, such as joining a local sports team, will help your young adult to manage their weight while providing relaxation and social opportunities and promoting good health. It may take a bit of encouragement, but if this is an option for your teenager, it's well worth considering.

The No-Diet Diet

Dieting isn't always necessary for weight loss. A few simple changes to what your teenager, and the rest of the family, are eating is often all it needs to boost their wellbeing.

- When preparing salads and vegetables, pick natural, uncomplicated seasonings like lemon, cider vinegar or extra virgin olive oil. These tend to contain fewer calories than mayonnaise and other bought salad dressings, and are healthier and tastier to boot.

- Try to keep preserved meat and overly salty foods off the menu. These can cause your teenager to eat more as foods high in salt can lead to cravings.

- Natural whole foods contain fewer calories and are generally healthier and tastier than takeaways and processed ready meals, which should be avoided.

- Talk openly about your reasons for choosing each meal, and work together as a family to eat well.

- Make a point of enjoying the food you eat.

- Mindful eating – when we really think about what we put in our mouths – has been shown to reduce calorie intake. If your teenager must snack as they surf the Internet, provide healthier options such as rice cakes, vegetable sticks and toasted seeds.

- Get active – the whole family can benefit from physical activity, which increases the amount of energy consumed by the body, as well as having health benefits. Weight is lost when we burn more energy than we consume, as the body uses fat deposits for fuel.

- Allow occasional treats. Encourage your teenager to eat something healthy before going out with friends, to reduce the risk of overeating. Encourage them to get back to eating healthily afterwards.

- Spend time reading labels before buying foods. Be aware that some low-fat foods have large amounts of sugar in them.

- Increase the amount of vegetables your teenager eats. Include orange, yellow and green options for good vitamin and mineral input.

How Do I Discuss Weight with My Teenager?

- Putting your teenager on a diet, criticising them too much or showing too much anxiety might cause disordered eating or a loss of confidence, so it's important that you're very careful when raising this matter.

- There is no set limit on how much a teenager should eat, so keep in mind that your child is unique. Before assuming they eat too much, give a great amount of consideration to their lifestyle, energy needs and diet.

- Don't rush the changes. It may be that your teenager is about to balance their ratio of height to weight through a growth spurt, and that their weight gain was just their body's way of preparing for this change.

- Explain what your concerns are and suggest ways your teenager might eat more healthily.

- If you feel your child's diet is healthy, you may want to encourage them to be more active. This doesn't have to mean sport – street dancing, skateboarding and walking will all burn energy.

Angela's Case Study: An Overweight Adolescent

Looking for advice on how to improve her diet, Francesca (aged 18) came to see me because she was obese. Francesca confessed to me that she did every diet around with poor results – after a few months the weight, and more, would go back on. An examination from her GP concluded that she had no underlying health problems, so she was unsure about the reasons for her weight gain. The doctor's recommendations were that she should exercise more and eat less. But every diet she tried just left her feeling hungry and miserable.

I asked her to limit the amount of calorie-dense, high sugar and fat foods she ate. This would keep her blood sugar level in balance for longer. I explained to Francesca that she could afford to indulge in what I call "socialising" foods for around 20% of her diet if the remaining 80% was balanced and healthy. Snacks should be fruit and crackers, rather than sweets and crisps. Whole grains like wheat, rice and oats with added fruit and seeds, for example, would make a healthier breakfast than white bread, butter and jam. Lean protein and lots of vegetables were a healthier option for dinner, and she could trade white pasta and cream sauces for whole grain pasta with tomato sauce, and replace chips with baked potatoes or roasted potatoes (using only a small amount of oil).

As Francesca enjoyed walking, I asked her to go out for a walk whenever she felt tense and tempted to reach for the biscuit barrel. I asked Francesca to keep a food diary to track her emotions as well as what she ate, as many people find this encouraging. Through this tool, she quickly realised that anxiety was a key trigger for eating, and that she tended to turn to food when she was put under pressure by her peers or her school. Within three months, Francesca had developed healthier ways to deal with stress and was well on her way to a healthier weight for her body type.

Summing Up

- The body of an adolescent is constantly growing and developing, and they need specific nutrients to deal with this.

- Foods that help to care for the complexion can really help with teenage skin problems.

- The development of hormones during puberty can be helped if your teen eats foods rich in certain nutrients.

- Eating disorders are particularly common in young people between the ages of 12 and 25.

- Family support and simple dietary changes can help to tackle the continuing problem of teenage obesity and overeating.

- You can plan menus to support your teenager during exam periods.

- Certain ingredients contain natural elements that can help to calm mood swings.

- A healthy diet at home can help to compensate for poor food choices elsewhere.

7

First Foods and Healthy Purées

What you give your child to eat in this first year can help to establish healthy eating patterns for life – it helps to instil an appreciation of fresh, nutritious produce; to teach manners and how to eat well; and to show that shared meals can be a special time for all the family. One of the most exciting times of your early parenthood will involve preparing their first purées and slowly introducing them to solid foods. With quick, inexpensive and foolproof options like these, you won't need to rely on processed jars of baby food.

Even if your carefully planned menus end up on the floor sometimes, watching your child explore new textures and flavours will always be a joy. However, first foods are about more than just the taste. The basics of preparing, cooking and selecting food for the first year of your child's life are discussed in Chapter Three. Some of the recipes below may just become your child's favourite food, so why not try them out?

A Note on the Recipes

- Unless it states otherwise, the recipes in this book will all make around six child portions. You can freeze portions or store them in the fridge for up to 24 hours if they aren't eaten immediately.

- Unless the recipe says to, you shouldn't add salt or sugar to these dishes.

- You'll find more nutrients in organic, free-range eggs and organic milk, so it's best to use these where possible.

- These dishes are suitable for the whole family, and it's easy to increase the quantities if needed. Once you have removed your child's portion from the pan, you can season your own food as much as you like.

- Wash all vegetables before cooking, scrubbing them with a brush to remove dirt and residues, if necessary.

- Use full fat milk. Avoid dairy products if your child is allergic or sensitive to them.

- Recipes containing only fruits and vegetables can be frozen for up to six months. Recipes with milk can be frozen for up to four weeks. Recipes with fish or meat can be frozen for up to 10 weeks.

Steamed, Boiled and Mashed Fruit and Vegetables

Your child's first purées will just be vegetables and fruit peeled and cooked so they can be mashed and eaten easily, and certain foods won't even need to be cooked first. Remember that preparing your child's food doesn't have to be a hassle – you can simply set aside some of the unseasoned, cooked vegetables you have prepared for your meal and whiz them in a blender or mouli to make a purée. Try avocado and banana for a speedy dish with no cooking needed.

It's a good idea to begin by giving your child just one type of purée per meal. Once they get used to this process, you can try experimenting with combined flavours to provide essential nutrients and more interesting flavours for your little one. Try these combinations – you can experiment with the balance of flavours or mix and match ingredients, depending on your child's tastes and what's in season.

- Banana and apple purée (great on its own or even mixed with plain yoghurt).

- Courgette, pea and kale purée (full of vitamin C and calcium).

- Sweet potato and basil.

- Sweet potato and pear.

- Avocado and mint purée (older toddlers can use this as a dip with pitta bread).

- Blueberry, apple and peach purée (great with yoghurt mixed in).

- Kiwi and melon.

- Butternut squash and sweet potato.

- Broccoli with mashed potato.

- Broccoli and cauliflower.

- Pea and mint.

When preparing purées, the mixture may come out a little thick, so it's a good idea to save some of the water used to cook the vegetables or boil and cool some water to thin it out.

Toddlers Aged between Seven and Nine Months

At this stage, you can start introducing protein into your child's daily menu. They'll find it easiest to digest things like chicken, white fish, lentils and turkey.

Cod and Corn Chowder

This chowder is a great source of energy and contains potassium, selenium and vitamin B12. It's perfect for older kids and babies alike. The poached fish stays super-moist, so it's really easy to turn into baby food!

This recipe makes 3 adult servings.

Ingredients

- 2 tablespoons of margarine or unsalted butter.

- 900 ml chicken stock.

- 1 lb of cod fillets, bones and skins removed.
- 250 ml whole milk.
- 2 cups of diced potatoes.
- 2 cups fresh or defrosted frozen corn kernel.

Optional Ingredients

- 1 medium onion, chopped.
- 2 cloves of garlic, chopped.
- 1 bay leaf.
- 1 pinch of black pepper.
- ½ tsp salt.
- 2 tsp chopped thyme.
- 1 cup chopped celery, (reserve leaves).

Method

1 Melt the butter in a large saucepan over medium heat.

2 Optional: Add the onion and celery and sauté until softened (around 4 minutes).

3 Increase the heat a little and add the corn (and thyme and garlic if using) and sauté until lightly golden (around 3 minutes). Add the stock and potatoes (and bay leaf) and bring to a boil.

4 Reduce the heat and simmer until the potatoes are slightly softened, but still firm in the centre (around 5 minutes). Add the milk and fish, and cook for a further 5 minutes or until the fish is cooked and the potatoes are soft. Use a fork to break the fish into chunks.

Italian Vegetable Pasta

Use mini pasta shapes, made for soup, in this recipe. Your child's immune system will be aided by the beta carotene found in red pepper and tomatoes.

Ingredients

- 200g tinned tomatoes, or fresh tomatoes that are peeled, chopped and deseeded.
- 1 small courgette, cubed.
- 25g mini pasta shapes.
- 175ml water.
- 1 red pepper, chopped.

Method

1 Over a medium heat, combine the pepper, water, courgette and tomatoes in a saucepan. Bring to the boil, then cover and reduce to a simmer for 15 minutes.

2 Use a blender to mix the sauce until smooth.

3 Add the pasta to a pan of boiling water and cook until soft (usually around 5-7 minutes).

4 Mix the pasta into the sauce.

> **'Pick and mix – replace the pasta with mashed potato.'**

Turkey and Tomato Purée

You'll find lots of superb nutrients for boosting your child's immunity in turkey, including zinc, iron, B vitamins and protein.

Ingredients

- 1 tablespoon of extra virgin olive oil.
- 2 small carrots, peeled and diced.
- 1 small turkey breast, chopped.
- 150ml water.
- 200g fresh tomatoes, peeled, deseeded and chopped, or tinned tomatoes.
- 100g potato, peeled and chopped.
- 25g onion, peeled and chopped.

Method

1 Over a medium heat, heat the olive oil in a saucepan. Use this to sauté and soften the carrot and onion.

2 Add the turkey and potato and sauté again for 5 minutes.

3 Add the water and the tomatoes. Bring the mixture to the boil, then reduce to a simmer until the potato is soft and the turkey cooked (around 30 minutes).

4 Mix in a blender. If necessary, you can thin the purée with a little boiled water.

Chicken and Rice Casserole Purée

This meal is packed with nutrients, including beta carotene, vitamin A and protein. This purée is sweet and gentle in flavour from its combination of carrot, rice and chicken.

Ingredients

- 50g whole grain rice.
- 1 chicken breast with the skin removed, cut into strips.
- 150g sweet potato, peeled and chopped.
- 50g fresh or frozen peas.
- 1 small carrot, peeled and chopped.
- 300ml water.

Method

1 Over a high heat, add the water, carrot, sweet potato, chicken and rice to a saucepan. Bring the mix to the boil, then reduce the temperature and allow it to simmer for around 30 minutes.

2 Add the peas and cook for another five minutes, or until the vegetables are tender and the chicken fully cooked (white all the way through).

3 Use a blender to mix to a purée, using some boiled and cooled water to thin the mixture if needed.

Lentil and Squash Purée

Young children can easily digest red lentils, which are high in iron and protein.

Ingredients

- 250g butternut squash.
- Low-salt vegetable stock.
- 50g red lentils (soaked for 30 minutes).

Method

1 Peel and deseed the squash, and cut into cubes.

2 Put the lentils and chopped squash into a small saucepan and cover them with vegetable stock.

3 Heat the pot to a simmer, and cook uncovered until the lentils and squash are soft (around 20 minutes).

4 Use a blender to mix to a purée, using some boiled and cooled water to thin the mixture if needed.

'Pick and mix – swap the lentils for cooked chickpeas.'

Pasta with Tomato and Plaice

Protect your child's immune defences with this rich source of protein, antioxidant vitamins and calcium.

Ingredients

- 1 skinned fillet of plaice.
- 150g of tinned tomatoes, or fresh tomatoes skinned, chopped and deseeded.
- 25g mini pasta shapes.
- 150ml milk.
- 1 tsp extra virgin olive oil.

Method

1 Preheat your oven to Gas Mark 4/180°C/350°F.

2 Arrange the plaice on an ovenproof dish, cover it with tomatoes and drizzle with olive oil. Add the milk and cover the dish with tin foil or a lid.

3 Bake this in the oven until the fish is cooked (around 20 minutes).

4 Cook the pasta in a pan of boiling water until soft (around 5-7 minutes).

5 Mash the tomatoes and fish together and stir in the pasta.

Toddlers Aged Nine to 12 Months

At this stage, your child will be able to eat a lot of the same foods that you can. This means you can enjoy mealtimes together by eating the same foods.

Beef Casserole

This dish combines a delicious mix of protein-rich beef and nutritious veggies.

Ingredients

- 2 tbsp extra virgin olive oil.
- 1 clove of garlic, minced.
- 1 tbsp all-purpose flour.
- 2 tsp dried basil.
- 200g chopped mushrooms.
- 450g potatoes, peeled and chopped.
- 1 tbsp tomato purée.
- 600ml water.
- 1 onion, chopped.
- 2 sticks of celery, chopped.
- 2 carrots, chopped.
- 350g braising beef, trimmed and cut into cubes.

Method

1 Preheat the oven to Gas Mark 3 (170°C/325°F).

2 Heat half of the oil in a casserole dish over a medium heat, and use it to sauté the beef. Remove this from the dish and set it aside.

3 Heat the remaining oil in the casserole dish over medium heat and sauté the onion and garlic until softened (around 5 minutes). Add the carrots and celery and cook for 5 minutes.

4 Place the beef back in the dish, and gradually stir in the flour. Add the water slowly before adding the tomato purée and herbs. Bring the mixture to the boil while stirring until the sauce begins to thicken.

5 Cover the dish and place it in the oven to bake for 90 minutes.

6 Add the potatoes and mushrooms and cook until the meat and potatoes are soft, usually around 30-40 minutes.

7 If necessary, you can mash or purée the casserole before serving.

Fish Pie

The fish and potato is a good combination of protein and carbohydrate. This is a meal for the whole family.

Ingredients

- 150g cod fillets, cut into chunks with the skin removed.
- 300ml whole milk.
- 125g onion, chopped.
- 25g all-purpose flour.
- 1 tbsp fresh parsley, chopped.
- 25g butter.
- 1 bay leaf.
- 150g salmon fillet, skinned and cut into chunks.

Topping

- 2 medium potatoes, peeled and chopped.
- 25g butter.
- 2 tbsp milk.
- 100g carrots, peeled and chopped.

Method

1 Preheat the oven to Gas Mark 4 (180°C/350°F).

2 In a saucepan over medium heat, add the milk, onion, bay leaf and fish. Bring it to the boil, then reduce to a simmer until the fish is cooked (8 minutes). Take the fish out of the pot, strain the milk and keep it to one side.

3 Over a medium heat, melt the butter in a saucepan. Stir in the flour until smooth. Add the reserved milk gradually while stirring constantly for a smooth sauce.

4 Break the fish into flakes and stir it – and the parsley– into the sauce. Pour this mixture into an ovenproof dish.

5 Place the carrots and potatoes into a saucepan and cover with water before bringing to the boil. Reduce to a simmer until the vegetables are softened, around 15-20 minutes. Drain the water away, add butter and milk and mash it all together.

6 Spread the potato and carrot mash over the fish mixture. Bake until golden, around 15-20 minutes.

Crispy Courgette and Carrot Bake

For vital nutrients and slow-release energy, you can't beat oats as a topping.

Ingredients

- 1 large courgette, grated.
- 125g onion, finely chopped.
- 1 tsp lemon juice.
- 250g carrots, grated.

Topping

- 50g porridge oats.
- 25g grated Parmesan.
- 4 tsp extra virgin olive oil.

Method

1 Preheat the oven to Gas Mark 4 (180°C/350°F).

2 Mix the carrots, lemon juice, onion and courgettes in a bowl. Pour the mixture into a casserole dish.

3 Mix the oil and oats in a bowl, and stir in the cheese.

4 Sprinkle the oat mixture over the vegetables in the dish. Bake until the topping is crisp and golden and the vegetables are soft, around 25 minutes.

Lentil and Spinach Purée

This dish is rich in protein and iron.

Ingredients

180g red lentils.

125g chopped onion.

180g spinach, frozen.

125ml coconut milk.

1 tsp mild curry powder.

1 tbsp extra virgin olive oil.

Method

1 Place the lentils in a saucepan and cover with water. Cook them over a medium heat until tender, around 20 minutes. When the lentils are cooked, drain away the water.

2 Over a medium heat, heat the olive oil in a saucepan. Add the onion and cook until softened, around 5 minutes.

3 Add the curry powder and cook for a further 2-3 minutes.

4 Stir in the lentils, coconut milk and spinach and bring to a boil. Reduce the temperature and simmer for around 10 minutes.

5 If necessary, you can purée this dish before serving.

Spinach and Salmon with Cheese Sauce

Salmon and other oily fish are great for developing brains. This fast-to-fix dish is also a great solution for children who are reluctant to eat spinach – with this tasty cheese sauce, they won't notice the difference!

Ingredients

- 25g butter.
- 250ml whole milk.
- 300g frozen spinach, chopped, defrosted and drained.
- 200g salmon fillet.
- ½ teaspoon salt.
- 1 tablespoon lemon juice.
- ⅔ cup shredded cheddar or shredded swiss cheese.
- 2 tablespoons all-purpose flour.

Method

1 Melt the butter in a large frying pan and stir in the flour until smooth.

2 Stir in the milk slowly, and bring it to a boil.

3 Cook until thickened (usually 1-2 minutes), stirring constantly.

4 Stir in the grated cheese until melted, and set this sauce to once side.

5 In a baking dish, lay out the spinach and sprinkle with lemon juice.

6 Lay the fish on the spinach and sprinkle with salt.

7 Pour the sauce over the top of the spinach and the fish.

8 Bake the dish uncovered at Gas Mark 4 (180°C/350°F) until the fish flakes easily with a fork, usually around 20-25 minutes.

Lentil and Lamb Stew

This delicious stew is full of fibre and protein. The cooking time for this dish is over 3 hours, so it's something you can set up in advance and leave until ready (this recipe makes 6 adult portions).

Ingredients

- 1 tbsp extra virgin olive oil.
- 200g carrot, peeled and chopped.
- 150g red lentils (soaked for 30 minutes).
- 1 litre of beef stock.
- Salt.
- 2 cloves.
- 2 sticks celery, chopped.
- 800g lamb on the bone.

Method

1 In a casserole dish or large pan, heat the olive oil and fry the lamb on each side until nicely browned. Take the lamb out of the pan and set to once side.

2 In the same oil, fry the chopped carrots and celery for 5 minutes before adding the lentils.

3 Put the meat back into the pan and pour in the stock along with the cloves.

4 Reduce the heat and allow the dish to simmer for around 3 hours, until the meat falls off the bone. If you notice the dish looking a little dry, feel free to add more stock.

5 Remove the meat from the bone, and serve with whole grain bread.

'Pick and mix – use lean beef instead of lamb.'

Summing Up

- Your child's first foods will introduce them to a world of new textures and flavours.

- You can avoid things like artificial flavourings and unnecessary chemicals by cooking dishes for your child using seasonal, nutritious and organic ingredients.

- Your child can learn vital social skills by eating homemade meals as a part of the family, and this can become a very special time to share together.

- Choosing healthy food options from the start can help to establish good eating habits for life.

- Homemade meals can be more economical than processed foods.

8

The Balanced Breakfast

Remember, a poor breakfast or no breakfast will have an effect on your child's school performance and, in the long run, on their body's overall nutritional balance. Of course, in the rush to get up and get ready for playgroup, school, or just the day ahead, it's easy to reach for the sugary cereal you know your child won't refuse. But your child is more likely to greet each day feeling strong, energetic and healthy if they have access to a good breakfast full of vital nutrients.

Take a look at the following recipes – children love them, and they're full of goodness and super speedy to prepare. For children who don't like to eat too much first thing, we've included a few basic smoothies that are easy on the tummy.

Commercial Cereals

Choose varieties that are low in sugar and salt. B vitamins, iron, calcium and other essential nutrients are found in many bought boxes of cereal, making them a good choice for kids. Add a handful of blackberries or a sliced ripe banana and some mixed seeds before serving with milk for an extra serving of potassium, antioxidants and essential fatty acids.

'Pick and mix – in winter, serve the pancakes with a warm compote of prunes and apricots that have been chopped and softened in a saucepan with 2 tbsp apple juice.'

A Note on the Recipes

- Unless it states otherwise, the recipes in this section serve four.
- You'll find more nutrients in free-range, organic eggs and organic milk, so use these if possible.
- Unless it states otherwise, don't bother adding salt or sugar to these recipes.
- Wash all vegetables before cooking, scrubbing them with a brush to remove dirt and residues, if necessary.
- Use full-fat milk if your child is five years or younger; semi-skimmed if older.

Breakfast Pancakes

Excluding the unavoidable hot frying pan, this pancake recipe is pretty kid-friendly. Who knows, maybe it'll be a new interest that they'll take up and look forward to doing with you! Encourage your children to mix the ingredients themselves. Depending on their ages, they might even be able to cook and flip the pancakes (with careful supervision). This is a great way to get your kids interested in preparing their own food. (This recipe makes 8 portions).

Ingredients

- 200g plain flour.
- ½ tsp vanilla essence.
- 300ml semi-skimmed milk.
- 1 egg.
- 2 tsp butter (melted).
- 3 tsp baking powder.

Method

1 Get all of your ingredients ready.

2 Add all dry ingredients (flour and baking powder, sugar and salt if needed) to a large mixing bowl. Make a small hollow in the centre of the ingredients.

3 Pour the milk, vanilla essence, egg and butter into the hollow.

4 Using a whisk, fork or electric mixer (on a low setting) to mix all the ingredients together. Scrape any flour from the side of the bowl and make sure it's fully mixed in.

5 Place the frying pan on a medium/high heat, and add some cooking spray or oil. If you have a griddle, this can be easier when it comes to flipping the pancakes.

6 Pour half a ladle of pancake batter into the frying pan to form a small pancake. Repeat as many times as you can, but make sure there's plenty of space around each pancake to make flipping easier.

7 Watch for small bubbles to form on the tops of each pancake. When a pancake is covered with bubbles, use a spatula to flip it over.

8 Cook the flipped pancake for another 30-45 seconds before removing them from the pan.

9 Serve with a range of healthy toppings like chopped fruits, lemon juice and honey.

'Pick and mix – add some strawberries or blueberries for extra vitamins.'

Banana Smoothie

It's breakfast in a glass and a great way to have a meal on the run. Full of bananas, yoghurt, cinnamon and moreish honey, this smoothie is a deliciously healthy way to start the day. (This recipe makes two portions).

Ingredients

- 400ml semi-skimmed milk.
- 8 tbsp plain yoghurt.
- 6 ice cubes.
- 1 tbsp honey.
- ½ tsp cinnamon.
- 2 bananas.

Method

1 Put all of the ingredients into your smoothie maker or blender – be sure to add the honey last.

2 Blend the mixture until all the lumps are gone.

3 Pour into two glasses, decorating with a slice of banana and a sprinkle of cinnamon on each.

Bio-Yoghurt with Seeds and Berries

The berries and seeds are full of nutrients, and the bacteria in the yoghurt will help digestion. If your child wants a change from cereal or is in a rush to get out the door, this light breakfast is the perfect solution. (This recipe makes 1 portion).

Ingredients

- 1 small pot or 5 tablespoons of plain yoghurt.
- 1 tbsp almonds, chopped.
- Handful of berries (raspberries, strawberries, blackberries or blueberries).
- 1 tbsp mixed seeds (sesame, pumpkin and sunflower).

Method

1 Put the yoghurt in a small dish and top it with the nuts, berries and seeds.

Boosted Oatibix

Yoghurt contains calcium, bacteria cultures, magnesium and vitamins B2 and B12. The seeds and wheatgerm are packed with more fantastic nutrients. Combine that with all the goodness of oats, and you're onto a winner. This breakfast will help to keep your child's blood sugar levels in balance through the magic of slow-release energy.

Ingredients

- 2 tablespoons of plain yoghurt.
- 4 portions of oatibix.
- 2 tablespoons of mixed seeds, including sunflower, pumpkin and sesame seeds.

- 1 handful per bowl of your child's favourite fruit, chopped.

- 2 tbsp almonds, chopped.

- 75g wheat germ.

- Milk, to cover.

Method

1 Place the Oatibix in four bowls, and add the milk and yoghurt.

2 Serve topped with the mixed seeds, fresh fruit, almonds and wheat germ.

Porridge with Mixed Fruits

This porridge can be made with seasonal, dried, frozen or fresh fruits, so choose whatever's on offer in your nearest supermarket. Be careful to check the label of each ingredients for allergy warnings. Save time when cooking this dish by leaving the apple unpeeled. It's really easy to cook porridge in the microwave, so long as you remember to stir it frequently.

If your child tends to be picky, feel free to change the recipe to include their favourite fruits instead of apricots. They may also prefer it made with milk instead of water.

Ingredients

- 80g dried apricots (around 10).

- 600ml water.

- 7 tablespoons porridge oats (100g).

- 2 apples (200g).

'Pick and mix – you could also use millet flakes or brown rice flakes instead of oats.'

Method

1 Wash the apples, remove their peel and cores and chop them into small chunks. Chop the apricots into small pieces.

2 Pour the water into a saucepan along with the oats. Bring this mixture to the boil for one minute, stirring constantly.

3 Reduce the heat to a simmer and add the apple and apricot pieces. Continue heating until the porridge is thick (around three minutes), stirring constantly.

4 Serve the porridge while it's nice and hot.

Easy Cheese Omelette

This omelette is perfect for breakfast, but can be eaten at any time of day. Your child will feel fuller for longer, and their muscles will get to grow and repair thanks to the affordable, delicious protein source that is the humble egg. For a balanced, healthy meal, serve your omelette with a simple tomato salad and/or some wholemeal bread. (This recipe makes 1 portion).

Ingredients

'Pick and mix – mix it up by adding tomatoes, spinach or goat's cheese as an alternative to Cheddar. Or serve poached or scrambled eggs instead of an omelette.'

- 2 free-range, organic eggs.
- 10g mild Cheddar cheese, grated.
- Olive oil.

Method

1 Break the eggs into a large bowl and add a pinch of salt and black pepper (if desired). Use a fork to beat the eggs until they're all one colour.

2 Warm up a small, non-stick frying pan on a low heat.

3 Pour a small amount of oil into the hot pan, and allow it to heat before adding the eggs.

4 Spread the eggs out evenly by tilting the pan gently.

5 When the eggs are beginning to cook but have not cooked all the way to the top, sprinkle the grated cheese on top of the omelette.

6 Unstick the omelette from the pan using a spatula, and fold one half over the other.

7 Remove the pan from the heat when the omelette begins to brown slightly underneath, and transfer the omelette to a plate.

Avocado on Oatmeal Toast

Serve this with a glass of milk for a great start to the day. Omega 6 fatty acids, B vitamins, potassium, zinc, folic acid and carotenoids can all be found in avocado. (This recipe makes 1 portion).

Ingredients

- 2 slices of toasted oatmeal bread.
- A small squeeze of lemon juice.
- ½ avocado.

Method

1 Remove the avocado from its peel, and mash it into a spreadable pulp. Spread this on your toast, with a small amount of lemon juice to taste.

Smoothie with Tropical Fruits

This is a real winner for children. It's full of slow-release energy, vitamin E and soluble fibre, and it tastes delicious! (This recipe makes 1 portion).

Ingredients

- 1 ripe mango or papaya, peeled, chopped and deseeded.
- 150ml water or orange juice.
- 2 bananas.

Method

1 Use your blender to whiz all of your ingredients together, and serve in a tall glass.

Summing Up

- For a good long-term nutritional balance and plenty of energy for the day ahead, try to give your child a healthy breakfast.

- Your child will have more energy for longer if they get a combination of carbohydrates and protein.

- Smoothies are a good option if your child doesn't like to eat a large breakfast.

- Fresh fruit and seeds can be added to commercial cereals to increase their nutrient content.

9

Kids Who Lunch

There are plenty of healthy sandwich ideas for your child's lunchbox in Chapter Five, but at the weekend when the whole family may have more time to eat together, it's possible you'll want to serve more than just sandwiches at lunchtime. Your child will have lots of energy for the afternoon's activities as well as a more stable blood sugar level if their meal includes protein as well as carbohydrates.

Rather than taking in their own food, many children in the UK eat lunches provided by their school cafeterias. Help them to pick the best options for a well-balanced plateful by talking to your child about the goodness that different types of food can provide.

Halloumi Kebabs

A deliciously fresh and salty meal on a stick comes to us through the magic of halloumi combined with fresh, organic vegetables.

Ingredients

- 3 tbsp olive oil.
- 450g halloumi cheese, cut into ¾-inch cubes.
- 8 cherry tomatoes.
- Wooden skewers, soaked in water for at least 30 minutes prior to use.
- 2 medium zucchini, cut into ½-inch rounds.
- 2 tablespoons fresh lemon juice from 1 lemon, plus 1 additional lemon cut into wedges for serving.

Method

1 In a large bowl, whisk together the oil and lemon juice. Add salt and cracked black pepper to taste.

2 Add the zucchini, tomatoes and cheese, and make sure everything is fully coated.

3 Thread these pieces onto skewers, making sure to leave enough empty skewer to use as a handle.

4 Over a barbecue or hot frying pan, or under a hot grill, grill the skewers until the cheese browns and the vegetables have softened slightly – this usually takes around 3-5 minutes on each side. Serve with lemon wedges.

Smoked Haddock Kedgeree

This dish shows us that flaky fish and boiled eggs are a match made in heaven! It's good for lunch, dinner or brunch.

Serves: Four.

Ingredients

- 2 free-range, organic eggs.
- Knob of butter.

- 1 small onion, chopped.
- 2 tbsp fresh parsley, chopped.
- Lemon wedges to serve.
- 4 tbsp double cream.
- 200g white basmati rice.
- 1 tsp groundnut or vegetable oil.
- 325g skinless boneless smoked haddock fillet.

Method

1 Place the eggs in a small pan of boiling water, and allow them to hard boil (around seven minutes). Remove the eggs from the water and cool under the tap or in a dish of cold water.

2 Place the haddock in a shallow pan and cover with cold water. Cover the pan with a lid and allow it to simmer until the fish flakes easily, around 8-10 minutes.

3 Melt the butter in a pan with the oil, and cook the onion until softened (8-10 minutes). Add the rice and cook for another two minutes.

4 Remove the fish from the water and set it on a plate. Add 600ml of the water used to cook the fish over the rice and onion and add a pinch of salt. Cover this and cook on low until the rice is tender, around 12 minutes.

5 Flake the fish into chunks, remove the eggs from their shells and cut them into quarters.

6 Carefully stir the cream, fish and most of the parsley into the rice. Add salt and pepper to taste, and top with the remaining parsley, lemon wedges and eggs.

Delicious Salmon

These simple Asian flavours are healthy and fresh, and we could all do with more fish in our diet. It'll take just 20 minutes to have this quick glazed salmon on the table.

Serves: Three.

Ingredients

- 80ml soy sauce.
- 3 salmon fillets.
- Lime wedges and coriander leaves to taste.
- 2 cups basmati rice.
- 4 tbsp brown sugar.

'Pick and mix – use cod instead of salmon, if you prefer, and choose whatever vegetables are in season.'

Method

1 Cut the salmon into chunks, and mix the soy sauce and brown sugar together.

2 Toss the salmon gently in the soy sauce and sugar mixture, and set to one side.

3 Put the rice in the saucepan with three cups of cold water, and bring it to the boil. Reduce the heat, cover the pan and allow it to cook for 12-14 minutes.

4 Line a baking tray with greaseproof paper, and set your grill to medium high.

5 Lay out the salmon pieces on the tray, and put this under the grill until the salmon is caramelised on top but still nice and pink inside (usually around six minutes).

6 Pour the remaining soy sauce and sugar marinade into a saucepan and allow it to simmer gently, reducing for a minute or so.

7 Spoon the rice into bowls, place some salmon pieces on top of the rice and drizzle the reduced marinade over the top. Serve with coriander leaves and a wedge of lime each.

Funghi e Riso (Mushrooms and Rice)

This meal is rich in iron, B vitamins, carbohydrates and protein. Excluding the unhealthy saturated fats, mushrooms contain many of the same nutrients found in meat.

Serves: Four.

Ingredients

- 400g whole grain or wild rice.
- 1 small onion, chopped.
- A small pinch of salt. Freshly ground black pepper to taste.
- 2 tbsp fresh parsley, chopped.
- 15 button mushrooms, wiped and finely sliced.
- 4 tbsp extra virgin olive oil.

Method

1 Add rice to a pan of boiled water and simmer until cooked (usually around 30 minutes). Drain the rice, setting a little of the cooking water to one side.

2 Over a medium temperature, heat the oil in a large saucepan. Add the mushrooms and onions, and sauté for 10 minutes, seasoning with the black pepper and salt.

3 Reduce the heat and add the cooked rice, along with a ladleful of the cooking water from the rice. Heat gradually until all of the water is absorbed, stirring occasionally.

4 Garnish each serving with a little chopped parsley.

Bistecca alla Pizzaiola (Steak with Tomatoes)

You can find iron and zinc in this dish, along with a great variety of other nutrients that your growing child needs.

Serves: Four.

Ingredients

- 2-3 tbsp extra virgin olive oil.
- 4 cloves garlic, finely sliced.
- A small pinch of salt.
- A handful of fresh, chopped parsley.
- Steamed broccoli, to serve.
- 8 large ripe tomatoes, peeled, deseeded and chopped.
- 1 small onion, chopped.
- 4 fillet steaks.

Method

1 Over a medium temperature, heat the oil in a frying pan. Add in the garlic, onion and steaks.

2 Cook the steaks until brown, around four minutes on each side. Remove it from the pan when cooked, and set it on a warm plate.

3 Use a pinch of salt to season the steaks, and keep them warm by covering with another plate.

4 Put the chopped tomatoes in the pan, and squash them gently with a fork. Cook over a low heat until a thick sauce forms. Put the steaks back in the pan with the tomatoes.

5 Add the chopped parsley, cooking for another five minutes.

6 Serve the steaks with a side of steamed broccoli.

'Pick and mix – swap the steak for turkey escalopes for a milder and more economical version of this dish.'

Ham and Tagliatelle Pasta

This recipe uses low-fat evaporated milk instead of cream for a healthier take on a family favourite. A creamy sauce is beloved by all.

Serves: Four.

Ingredients

- 350g tagliatelle pasta.
- 2 cloves garlic, finely sliced.
- 200g peas, cooked.
- 375ml low-fat evaporated milk.
- ½ cup finely grated parmesan cheese.
- 1 bunch English spinach, washed and chopped.
- 150g lean leg ham, sliced.
- 1 onion, sliced.

Method

1 Follow the directions on the packet to cook the tagliatelle, and drain away the water.

2 In a non-stick pan, sauté the onion and garlic with a little water until the onion is soft.

3 Add the ham and peas, and cook until heated through (add more water if necessary).

4 Add the spinach and cook until wilted.

5 Pour in the evaporated milk, and bring to the boil.

6 Remove the mixture from the heat, and mix with the pasta.

7 Serve topped with Parmesan cheese.

'Pick and mix – use inexpensive salmon offcuts, available from supermarkets, instead of the ham.'

Speedy Pasta

A really easy recipe for spaghetti with tomato sauce, super-quick to prepare and popular with the kids.

Serves: Four (or six young children).

Ingredients

- Knob of butter.
- 1 onion, chopped.
- 800g tinned chopped tomatoes.
- 20 capers, chopped very finely.
- Salt and pepper to taste.
- ½ tsp dried oregano.
- 1 large carrot, finely chopped.
- ½ tbsp oil.

Method

1 Melt the butter in a pan with the oil. Add the chopped onion and cook on a medium heat until it starts to soften, usually around 2-3 minutes.

2 Add the carrots and fry for another few minutes, stirring occasionally.

3 Add the dried oregano, capers and tomatoes, and mix it all together.

4 Allow the mixture to simmer for 10-12 minutes. Remove it from the heat and mix with cooked spaghetti.

5 Add salt and pepper to taste, and serve.

Potato and Lentil Soup

This soup's perfect balance of carbohydrates, iron and protein makes it a complete meal.

Serves: 4-6.

Ingredients

- 350g brown lentils, soaked overnight.
- 2 cloves garlic, finely sliced.
- 2 slices of bacon with the rind removed.
- 3 medium potatoes, cubed.
- Salt and pepper to taste.
- 2 slices wholemeal bread, crusts removed and cut into cubes.
- 2 carrots, sliced.
- 1 tin of tomatoes or 4 ripe tomatoes, sliced.
- 1 small onion, peeled and finely chopped.
- 4 tbsp olive oil.

Method

1 Rinse the soaked lentils in cold water several times.

2 On a medium setting, heat 1 tbsp of oil in a saucepan. Add the bacon, onion and garlic and cook for five minutes.

3 Add the lentils, potatoes and tomatoes with enough water to cover them. Season with salt and black pepper.

4 Cover the soup and cook until the potatoes and lentils are tender, usually around 35 minutes.

5 Add the remaining 3 tbsp oil to a frying pan over a medium heat. Make croutons by frying the cubes of bread until golden. Remove these from the pan, and use kitchen towel to drain excess oil.

6 Sprinkle the croutons on the soup, and serve.

Ricotta Sauce with Tortellini

A good mix of protein and carbohydrate. Replace your usual cheese sauce with a soft, sweet ricotta.

Serves: Four.

Ingredients

- 3 tbsp extra virgin olive oil.
- A small handful of torn, fresh basil leaves.
- 500g tortellini pasta.
- 2 tbsp grated Parmesan cheese.
- 300g ricotta.
- Pinch of salt.
- 500g ripe tomatoes or 1 tin of tomatoes.

Method

1 Heat the oil in a saucepan over a medium heat. Add the basil, salt and tomatoes and cook for 20-30 minutes.

2 Follow the instructions on the packet to cook the tortellini, draining away excess water when cooked.

3 Sieve the ricotta and add it to the cooked tomato sauce, stirring to combine fully.

4 Add the cooked tortellini, covering every piece with sauce.

5 Serve sprinkled with Parmesan.

Fish Fingers with a Twist

Children will love this healthy combination of fish and oats.

Ingredients

- 350g haddock or another white fish, cut into "fingers".
- 25g rolled oats.
- 2 tbsp extra virgin olive oil.
- Salad or green vegetables, to serve.
- 1 egg.
- 25g wholemeal breadcrumbs.

Method

1 Preheat your oven to Gas Mark 3 (170°C/325°F).

2 In a bowl, mix together the breadcrumbs and oats. Crack and whisk the egg in a different bowl.

3 Dip each piece of fish into the egg, before covering it in the oat and breadcrumb mix.

4 Heat the oil in a frying pan over a medium heat. Cook the fish strips on each side until golden brown.

5 Lay the fish fingers out on a baking tray, and bake for 10 minutes.

6 Serve with steamed green vegetables or a side salad.

Summing Up

- A light cooked lunch is great when you have the time – your child needs to eat something other than sandwiches!

- Children love pasta, and it's a very quick and filling meal.

- Fish is a nutrient-packed alternative to meat.

- Combining protein with carbohydrates means energy is released more slowly.

10

Dinner for the Whole Family

One of the best times to eat, relax and enjoy time together as a family is at dinnertime. It's not always easy to get everyone to sit down at once, though! Aim to eat as a family at some point in the week – it doesn't have to be dinner; a weekend lunch or daily breakfast are brilliant times to catch up over a joint enjoyment of food. Try to sit with your child while they eat their dinner, even if there isn't time to share a meal.

While it's often better to eat a larger meal at lunch, when we're more likely to move around and use up the energy we've consumed, and our digestive system is more active, dinner is the main meal of the day in many families. When your child is tired in the evening, a healthy soup is really easy to digest and eat. Soups are full of nutrients and so diverse and delicious, they can make the perfect dinner for the whole family.

Haddock Gratin

This is a delicious alternative to fish pie. The ingredients are inexpensive, and it's really quick to prepare.

Ingredients

- 1.5kg haddock fillets (undyed).
- 500ml water.
- 3 tbsp double cream.
- Wholegrain rice or boiled potatoes to serve.
- 4 tbsp wholemeal breadcrumbs.
- 500g broccoli, steamed.
- 500ml milk.

'Pick and mix – use unsmoked fish, such as salmon and cod and swap spinach or shredded cabbage for the broccoli.'

Method

1 Preheat the oven to Gas Mark 6 (200°C/400°F).

2 Carefully remove any bones from the haddock. Place the fillets in a shallow pan, covering with water and milk.

3 Bring the liquid to a boil over a high heat, then reduce the temperature and simmer until the fish is cooked through and tender (5-10 minutes).

4 Take the fish out of the cooking liquid.

5 Place the steamed broccoli in a shallow baking dish. Remove the skin from the fish and flake it into the dish. Pour over the double cream, followed by the breadcrumbs.

6 Bake until the dish is bubbling, around 25 minutes. Serve with boiled potatoes or wholegrain rice.

Creamy Risotto

If you want to boost your child's developing immune system, you can't go wrong with this vitamin-rich dish. Your child will love creating the vegetable decorations around the side of the plate, and it's so easy to prepare and eat.

Serves: Four.

Ingredients

- 350g arborio rice.
- 150g peas, cooked.
- 2 tbsp extra virgin olive oil.
- 1 garlic clove, chopped.
- 240ml jar of passata (pulped tomatoes).
- 240ml single cream.
- Salt and freshly ground black pepper.
- 1 stick celery, finely chopped.
- 1 onion, chopped.
- 100g Brussels sprouts or runner beans.
- 2 carrots.

Method

1 Follow the packet instructions to boil the rice (usually around 30-40 minutes).

2 Boil or preferably steam the peas, runner beans, Brussels sprouts and carrots until slightly softened. Chop the carrots into cubes when cooked.

3 Set the vegetables to one side.

4 Over a medium heat, pour 1 tablespoon of olive oil into a small saucepan. Sauté the garlic, celery and onion until softened, around 3-4 minutes.

5 Sprinkle in the salt and pepper and the passata and allow to cook for another 10-15 minutes. If necessary, you can add boiled water to thin the sauce.

6 Use a blender to liquidise the sauce, then stir in the single cream. Put the sauce back in the saucepan and allow it to heat through for 2-3 minutes.

7 Stir two-thirds of the vegetables into the cooked rice in a large serving bowl. Drizzle olive oil over the top.

8 Serve with the sauce on the side, and use the remaining vegetables to create decorations for the sides of each plate.

Pollo alla Cacciatore (Hunter's Chicken Stew)

Children and adults alike will love this flavoursome mixture of vegetables and protein.

Serves: Six.

Ingredients

- 4 tbsp extra virgin olive oil.
- A medium chicken, seasoned with salt and pepper and separated into pieces.
- 1 onion, sliced.
- 390g (1 tin or carton) of chopped tomatoes.
- Wholegrain rice or boiled potatoes to serve.
- Steamed leafy green vegetables and carrots, to serve.
- Handful fresh rosemary and parsley, chopped.
- 120ml white wine.
- 1 garlic clove, chopped.
- 1 knob of butter.

Method

1 Preheat your oven to Gas Mark 4 (180°C/350°C).

2 In a frying pan, heat the oil and butter and use it to sauté the chicken pieces until golden. Remove the chicken and set to one side.

3 Place the onion and garlic in the pan and sauté until tender.

4 Place the pan over a medium heat and put the chicken back in with the onions and garlic. Add the wine and stir continuously until it evaporates.

5 Transfer the chicken, onions and garlic to an ovenproof dish and add the tomatoes and herbs.

6 Cook in the oven until the chicken is cooked through, usually around an hour. Check the chicken is fully cooked by sticking the point of a knife into one piece and seeing if the juices run clear.

7 Serve with vegetables and potatoes or rice.

Tagliatelle con la Trota (Tagliatelle with Trout)

Trout is rich in essential fatty acids, and kids love its delicate flavour.

Ingredients

- 4 tbsp extra virgin olive oil.
- 4 fillets of trout, washed.
- 600g large tomatoes, peeled, seeds removed and chopped.
- 1 teaspoon salt.
- 2 tbsp fresh parsley, chopped.
- 400g egg tagliatelle.
- 3 courgettes, sliced.
- 200ml vegetable stock.
- 1 onion, sliced.

Method

1 Heat the oil in a saucepan at a medium setting. Place the chopped onion in the oil and sauté until softened, around 5 minutes.

2 Add the salt, trout fillets, tomatoes, courgettes and stock. Allow this to simmer gently until the sauce begins to thicken, around 15 minutes.

3 Follow the packet instructions to cook the tagliatelle, drain away the water and place in a large bowl to serve.

4 Pour over the trout sauce and serve sprinkled with parsley.

'Pick and mix – use fresh tuna as an alternative to trout.'

Chicken Soup

If your child has a cold or respiratory problems, the garlic and onion in this soup might be helpful.

Serves: 4-6.

Ingredients

- 4-6 skinned chicken thighs.
- 2 sticks of celery, chopped.
- 4 cloves garlic, finely sliced.
- 1 teaspoon salt.
- 200g broccoli or runner beans, cut into pieces.
- 2 litres of water.
- 1 small onion, peeled and chopped.
- 1 carrot, peeled and chopped.

Method

1 Into a large saucepan, combine all ingredients except for the runner beans or broccoli. Bring the mixture to the boil, before reducing the heat, covering the pot and allowing it to simmer for 45 minutes.

2 Using a slotted spoon remove the chicken thighs from the soup. Take the meat off the bones.

3 Cut the meat into small pieces and put it back into the saucepan.

4 For the last 5 minutes, add the runner beans or broccoli to the soup.

Carrot and Leek Soup

Children love this sweet and colourful soup.

Serves: Eight.

Ingredients

- 2 tbsp extra virgin olive oil.
- 1 litre of water.
- 6 large carrots, peeled and sliced.
- 230ml heavy whipping cream.
- 2 teaspoon salt.
- 6 large potatoes, diced.
- 4 leeks, chopped.

Method

1 Over a medium-high heat, cook the oil in a stock pot. Add the leeks and stir until softened, usually around four minutes.

2 Pour the water into the pot and add the carrots, salt and potatoes.

3 Bring the soup to the boil and cook until the carrots and potatoes are soft, around 20 minutes.

4 Blend the soup until it's completely smooth. Stir in the cream, reduce the heat and simmer until the soup thickens slightly, around 20 minutes.

'Pick and mix – add 150g cooked wholegrain rice to the soup to make a more complete meal.'

Prawny Spaghetti

You'll find plenty of iron, omega 3 fatty acids, vitamin B12, zinc and protein in a plate of prawns. As they can cause an allergic reaction, it's best not to serve this dish to children under the age of five.

Serves: Four.

Ingredients

- 400g spaghetti.
- 6 tbsp extra virgin olive oil.
- 300g prawns.
- 300g large tomatoes, peeled, seeds removed and chopped.
- 2 tbsp fresh parsley, chopped.
- 1 lemon.
- 1 small wine glass white wine (all the alcohol cooks away, so don't worry!)
- 1-2 dried red chillies.
- 2 cloves garlic.

Method

1 Following packet instructions, cook the spaghetti in a large pan of salted boiling water.

2 Peel the garlic and chop it finely. Heat the oil in a large frying pan and add the chilli and garlic.

3 Add the prawns when the garlic begins to brown, and sauté them briefly. Add the tomato purée and white wine, and allow the mixture to simmer for a few minutes.

4 Check that the pasta is ready, and drain it, making sure to set aside a little of the cooking water. Grate the zest from the lemon.

5 Add the spaghetti to the sauce and toss it together. Add the lemon juice, half of the parsley, and a small amount of the pasta cooking water to thin out the sauce a little. Season to taste.

6 Serve topped with parsley and lemon zest.

Meat & Tomato Pasta Sauce

If you have a slow cooker, this is the perfect ragu recipe to prepare for your kids. Its simple flavours are popular with most hungry tummies, and it's full of nutrients for a great family meal!

Serves: Four.

Ingredients

- 600g minced beef.
- 2 large carrots, peeled and sliced.
- 1 tbsp tomato purée.
- 2 cloves garlic, chopped.
- 80ml water.
- 2 tsp mixed dried herbs.
- 1 beef stock cube.
- 2 celery sticks, finely chopped.
- 390g (1 tin or carton) of chopped tomatoes.

Method

1 Cook all of the ingredients together in the slow cooker for 7 hours.

2 Towards the end of the cooking time, use a fork or masher to break up the meat so it can mix with the sauce. Feel free to add more water if you feel it's needed.

3 Serve with vegetables and pasta.

Kid-Made Pizza

This recipe is super-simple so even your small children will be able to join in. Lots of kids love to choose their own ingredients and shape their dough themselves.

Serves: Two.

Ingredients

- 250g strong white bread flour, plus extra for dusting.
- 1 tsp salt.
- 1 tbsp extra virgin olive oil.
- 300ml water.
- 1 teaspoon dried active baking yeast.
- Toppings:
- 200ml jar of passata (pulped tomatoes).
- Prosciutto or other ham, sliced.
- 1 red pepper, chopped.
- Olives.
- Mushrooms.
- Mozzarella cheese, sliced or grated.

'Pick and mix – try different combinations of toppings, such as spinach and egg; tomato, olive and mozzarella; courgette, aubergine and olive; and ham and ricotta.'

Method

1 Mix the yeast, salt and flour. Add the olive oil and water and stir (feel free to add a little more flour if the dough is too sticky).

2 Roll the dough into a ball, wrap it in cling film and leave it to rest for 10 minutes.

3 Preheat the oven to Gas Mark 6 (200°C). Cover a baking tray in flour, and roll out the dough.

4 Spread the tomato sauce on the base and add the cheese with any other toppings your child fancies.

5 Put the pizza in the oven for 15 minutes, or until the pizza base is puffy and golden.

Brain Food (Fishcakes)

You can make fishcakes from any pre-cooked fish – try them with smoked mackerel, or tinned tuna or salmon! If you can't find pre-cooked fish, you could also cook a fillet of fish yourself and allow it to cool.

Ingredients

- 175g potato, cooked and mashed.
- 1 lemon.
- 100g breadcrumbs or crushed cream crackers.
- 1 tbsp vegetable or sunflower oil.
- Freshly ground black pepper.
- 200g/7oz cooked fish – use either smoked mackerel or a tin of tuna or salmon.

Method

1 Preheat the oven to Gas Mark 7 (220°C/425°F).

2 Wash the potatoes and boil with skins on until soft (usually around 20-30 minutes). Rinse and leave to cool.

3 Mash the cooked potatoes.

4 Add the fish and give it a good mix. Add the black pepper and the juice of the lemon, with any other seasoning you fancy.

5 Taste the mixture to see if it needs any more seasoning – it's already cooked, so it's safe!

6 With wet hands, roll the fishcake mixture into small bowls. Coat these in crushed crackers or breadcrumbs.

7 Pour the oil into a baking tray, spreading so it covers the bottom, and place the fishcakes on the oily tray. Flip them over once so that both sides have a little oil.

8 Put the fishcakes in the preheated oven.

9 Allow the fishcakes to bake for 10 minutes. Turn the cakes over, then bake until they're golden-brown, usually another 10 minutes.

10 Use kitchen towel to drain any extra oil from the fishcakes before serving.

Summing Up

- As often as possible, try to eat your meals together as a family. Sit at the table with your child when they eat, even if you aren't eating yourself.

- Choose soup for a nutrient-rich dinner that's easy for your child to digest.

- If you have a big freezer, make extra portions of sauces and soups so you can have them again.

- Choose meals your child can help to make, such as pizza or risotto.

- It's often better to have a larger lunch than dinner.

11

Treats and Nibbles

Unless there is a medical reason not to, giving your child the occasional treat is absolutely fine. Between-meal snacks are sometimes necessary to provide the extra calories and goodness your child needs to keep them on the go – they may have small stomachs, but they use up a LOT of energy! Providing homemade snacks and treats, rather than bought and processed ones, will also help your child to grow accustomed to healthier options. If you want to reduce irritability and mood swings, you'll also need a snack food that can help to balance your child's blood sugar levels.

However, do keep in mind that your child won't be able to eat their proper meals if you give them too many snacks. See Chapter Five for some speedy snack ideas, and check out the recipes below.

Well Cool Ice Lollies

Topped with rich dark chocolate and crunchy cereal for a moreish frozen treat, these easy fruity lollies count as one of your child's five-a-day.

Ingredients

- 2 ripe mangoes with the peels and stones removed, chopped roughly.
- 140ml coconut milk.
- 100g dark chocolate, broken up.
- 100g granola.
- 2 large ripe bananas, peeled and roughly chopped.

Method

1 Use a blender to mix the banana, mango and coconut milk into a smooth, thick liquid. Pour this into lolly moulds and leave in the freezer overnight.

2 When the lollies are frozen, break up the granola so there aren't any large lumps (you could use a food processor for this) and pour into a bowl.

3 Place a bowl over the pan, not allowing it to touch the boiling water. Put the dark chocolate into the bowl.

4 Allow the dark chocolate to melt, stirring with a wooden spoon. Be careful that you don't overheat it.

5 Take the lollies out of the moulds and dip each one into the chocolate, followed by the granola.

6 Lay them out on a plate or tray and allow them to set (this won't take long)!

7 Eat immediately, or put them back in the freezer until you want them.

Pear Tart

Your child will only need a small slice of this tart. It will stay fresh for three or four days if you store it in an airtight tin.

Ingredients

- 45g butter, softened.
- ¾ tsp cinnamon.
- 35g chopped walnuts
- ¾ cup all-purpose flour.
- ½ cup sugar.
- Filling:
- 225g reduced-fat cream cheese.
- 1 egg.
- 425g pears, peeled, cored and sliced.
- ¼ teaspoon ground cinnamon.
- 1 teaspoon vanilla extract.
- ¼ cup plus 1 tablespoon sugar, divided.

'Pick and mix – use slices of apple, instead of pear, to make the tart filling.'

Method

1 Preheat the oven to 220°C (425°F). Mix the sugar and cinnamon into the butter until crumbly.

2 Mix the walnuts and flour into the butter mixture. Grease a pie tin and press the mixture into the bottom and up the sides.

3 Beat the ¼ cup of sugar into the cream cheese until smooth for the filling. Mix in the vanilla extract and egg.

4 Spread the filling in the pie crust, and arrange the pear slices on the top.

5 Mix the remaining sugar with ¼ teaspoon of cinnamon and sprinkle this over the pears.

6 Bake the tart for 10 minutes. Reduce the heat to 175°C (350°F) and bake for another 15-20 minutes, or until the filling is set.

7 Transfer the tart to a wire rack and allow it to cool for an hour. Place the tart in the fridge and allow it to cool for another 2 hours before serving.

Carrot Biscuits

These biscuits are delicious and so quick and easy to bake.

Makes 36 biscuits.

Ingredients

- 115g butter, softened.
- 1 egg, whisked.
- 1 tsp vanilla essence.
- 300g plain flour.
- Pinch of sea salt.
- ¾ cup raisins.
- 1 ½ tsp bicarbonate of soda.
- 1 cup brown sugar.
- 1 cup carrot mashed.
- ½ cup sugar.

Method

1 Preheat the oven to 180°C, and lightly grease an oven tray.

2 Beat the butter and sugar together into a cream, and add the carrot, vanilla and egg.

3 Sieve the flour, and mix all the dry ingredients together. Add these to the wet mixture and stir until smooth. Mix in the raisins.

4 Lay out spoonfuls of the mixture on the greased baking tray and bake for 15 minutes.

Potato Croquettes

The cheese in this recipe gives these snacks a boost of protein, while the potatoes are rich in carbohydrates. Once cooked, these can be eaten warm or cold.

Makes 12-15 croquettes.

Ingredients

- 600g potato, cooked and mashed.
- 50g pecorino and 50g parmesan cheese.
- 1 tbsp fresh parsley, chopped.
- 1 egg yolk.
- Coating:
- Small amount of plain flour.
- 100g breadcrumbs or crushed cream crackers.
- Extra virgin olive oil, for frying.
- 1 egg, beaten.

Method

1 Stir the cheese, parsley and egg yolk into the mashed potato.

2 Roll this mixture into small sausage shapes and allow them to firm up in the fridge for at least 20 minutes.

3 Give the croquettes a light coating of flour, dip them in the egg and roll in breadcrumbs until fully coated.

4 Over a medium setting, heat the olive oil in a saucepan and fry the croquettes until golden. Drain cxccss oil using kitchen paper before serving.

Hummus at Home

This is a delicious dip from the Middle East. It's great with fresh carrots, cucumbers and peppers, or strips of pitta bread. It's also great as a spread in sandwiches.

Ingredients

- 1 tin chickpeas, drained (reserve 2-3 tbsp water from the tin).
- Pinch of sea salt.
- 2 tsp ground cumin.
- 3 tbsp extra virgin olive oil.
- 1 tsp paprika.
- ½ cup water.
- ¼ cup lemon juice.
- ¼ teaspoon pepper.
- 2 large cloves of garlic peeled and crushed.

Method

1 Place all the ingredients (except for the paprika and water) into a blender.

2 Mix everything until it is smooth and creamy (if your blender has a purée setting, this is the one to use). If it's too thick, gradually add water until it's soft enough for dipping.

3 Decant the hummus into a shallow bowl, drizzle with olive oil and sprinkle with paprika.

Carrot Cream with Herby Scones

The creamy carrot filling works great with these scones, but you can also eat them plain or with buttcr.

Ingredients

- 225g self-raising flour, plus extra for dusting.
- ¼ tsp caster sugar.

- 1 tbsp chopped fresh thyme.
- 4 ½ tbsp plain yoghurt.
- 25ml milk, plus extra for brushing.
- 1 egg, beaten.
- 1 tbsp fresh parsley, chopped.
- 60g butter, cubed.
- Filling:
- 1 small carrot, grated.
- Zest from half an orange.
- 100g cream cheese.
- 1 tbsp orange juice.

'Pick and mix – try plain cream cheese with the herby scones, or use grated beetroot instead of the carrots.'

Method

1 Preheat the oven to Gas Mark 7 (220°C/425°F).

2 Into a bowl, sieve the flour. Use your fingertips to rub in butter until the mixture looks like breadcrumbs.

3 Stir in the herbs and sugar, followed by the yoghurt, milk and egg.

4 Roll the dough into a ball, then press out on a floured surface until it's around 2cm thick.

5 Cut the scones out with a small, round cutter and lay them out on a baking tray, brushing each one with a little milk.

6 Bake until risen and golden, around 10-12 minutes, and cool on a wire rack.

7 Stir the orange juice, zest and grated carrot together in a bowl. Add the cream cheese and mix thoroughly.

8 Cut the scones in half, and serve spread with the carrot cream.

Soft & Smooth Baked Apples

Made with vitamin-rich fresh and dried fruits, these make a perfect pudding or larger afternoon snack.

Ingredients

- 5 tbsp raisins.
- 1 tsp cinnamon.
- 4 medium cooking apples, cores removed.
- 4 tsp honey.

Method

1 Preheat the oven to Gas Mark 5 (190°C/375°F).

2 Mix the honey, cinnamon and raisins together in a bowl.

3 Place the apples in a shallow baking dish and spoon the raising mixture into their middles.

4 Pour 2 tablespoons of hot water into the dish and bake until soft, around 30 minutes. These can be eaten warm or cold.

Homemade Chocolate Whip

This homemade chocolate mousse is far healthier than many bought versions, as it's free from artificial flavours, added sugars and thickeners.

Ingredients

- 125g dark chocolate, broken up.
- 4 eggs, separated into yolks and whites.
- 50g white chocolate, grated.
- 30g unsalted butter.

Method

1 Over a medium heat, pour a few centimetres of water into a small saucepan. Switch off the heat when the water boils.

2 Place a bowl over the pan, not allowing it to touch the boiling water. Put the butter and dark chocolate into the bowl.

3 Allow the dark chocolate to melt, stirring with a wooden spoon. Be careful that you don't overheat it.

4 Beat the egg yolks and gradually add them to the chocolate mixture.

5 Whisk the egg whites until they're fluffy and white. Fold them into the chocolate mixture carefully.

6 Divide the mousse into small bowls or cups, and put in the fridge for two hours to chill.

7 Serve sprinkled with white chocolate.

Strawberry Yoghurts

Flavoured yoghurts can be quite unhealthy, so these are a great alternative. If your child is under one, leave out the honey.

'Pick and mix – try crushed blueberries or raspberries instead of strawberries.'

Ingredients

- 400g crushed strawberries, with extra berries to decorate.

- 2 tsp honey.

- 450g thick Greek yoghurt.

Method

1 Gently mix the yoghurt, honey and strawberries together (don't mix them fully if you want a pattern of pink and white).

2 Serve in bowls, decorated with chopped strawberries.

Summing Up

- Energy and goodness will be provided by a healthy, wholesome snack. They can also serve to keep your child's blood sugars balanced.

- Your child may develop a taste for healthier options if you help them to make their own treats and snacks.

- Bear in mind that constant snacking will reduce your child's appetite for main meals.

- The occasional treat is fine to eat, unless your child has a medical problem.

12

Food as Medicine

When your child is feeling poorly, a warming meal can be just what the doctor ordered. And food can sometimes be more than just comforting! You can boost your child's wellbeing by following the suggestions in this chapter, power-packed prescriptions for all maladies. Keep in mind that the suggestions we make in this chapter are generalised and should not be used in place of professional medical advice.

Acne

As we discussed in Chapter Two, a diet rich in omega 3 foods can do wonders for skin problems.

- Omega 3 essential fatty acids are found in high quantities in oily fish like sardines, fresh tuna and salmon.
- Omega 3 can also be found in dark leafy green vegetables.
- Your child's skin will thank them for eating soups like minestrone, which are rich in vitamins and minerals.

- Skin health can be improved by cutting down on foods high in salt and sugar, so it's a good idea to cut down on your child's intake of fried and processed foods, and simple carbohydrates.

- Zinc-rich foods, such as fish, lean red meat, poultry, dairy products, wholegrain rice and nuts and seeds are important for healthy skin, especially during puberty.

- Choose foods that are rich in fibre, such as wholegrain bread and fruit.

- Seeds such as flaxseed, pumpkin and walnuts are also rich in omega 3 – sprinkle them on breakfast cereals and salads, or give to your child as a tasty snack.

Earache

Always consult a GP if you are worried about your child's ear pain. Some people seem to produce more mucus when exposed to certain foods. It may be worth avoiding these foods if your child has an earache.

- Serve lots of fresh fruit and vegetables to increase your child's intake of antioxidants.

- Replace sugary drinks and fruit juices (apart from pineapple) with water. The bacteria causing the problem can be fed by the sugars in sugary drinks.

- Pineapple juice may help to thin the secretion of mucus.

- Avoid dairy products and fatty foods, as these may cause excess mucus production.

Nosebleeds

Children tend to be very prone to recurrent nosebleeds. During a cold, your child is even more likely to experience nosebleeds as the nasal membrane will be more delicate than normal and blood vessels can be damaged by nose blowing.

- Vitamin C can help strengthen your child's capillaries while vitamin K is good for blood clotting. Both of these can be found in green vegetables.

- However, consult a GP if you're worried about your child's nosebleeds.

Coughs and Colds

You can boost your child's immune system and help stop their sniffles with the following foods:

- Chicken Soup (full recipe in chapter 10) is packed with great nutrients. Soups containing onion and garlic can also support your child's respiratory system.

- Cow's milk can increase mucus levels. Avoid this by using soya milk instead.

- Your body can create vitamin A from the beta carotene found in dark green vegetables and carrots. These foods are also full of zinc and vitamin C, which are great for the immune system.

- Sinus congestion can be reduced by tea tree pollen, which is found in manuka honey. 1 tsp of honey with a slice of lemon and hot water will make a tasty, healing hot drink for your child. If your child is under the age of one, do not give them honey.

- Garlic has antibacterial properties and can be added to many different meals.

- Give citrus fruit or juice, which is rich in vitamin C and can help to boost immunity.

- Sprinkle wheat germ on salads or breakfast. It's rich in vitamins B and E, zinc, magnesium and iron to boost wellbeing.

Dermatitis

Also known as eczema, children can find this itchy skin condition very distressing.

- You can find skin-supporting antioxidants and beta carotene in freshly squeezed carrot, mango and papaya juice, which you can alternate from day to day to keep it interesting.

Cold Sore

The symptoms of cold sores can be worsened by the amino acid arginine. Foods like chicken, wheat cereals, almonds, bacon, chocolate and peanuts all contain this amino acid. Meanwhile, the cold sore virus may be inhibited by lysine, another amino acid. You may reduce the occurence of cold sores by giving your child more foods that are high in lysine and avoiding those that contain arginine.

- Arginine can be found in peanut butter, fried foods, nuts and seeds, chocolate, butter and white flour products, so it's a good idea to cut back on these.

- High levels of lysine can be found in dairy products, eggs and soya foods.

- Lysine-rich foods include fish, red meat, chicken and turkey, watercress and beans.

Iron Deficiency

Also known as anaemia, iron deficiency can be combated by consuming iron-rich foods.

- Raisins, brown rice, poultry, eggs, beets and figs are all good foods for your child to try.

- Include plenty of green leafy vegetables. These contain vitamin C, which aids iron absorption.

Recipes

Immunity-Booster Soup

This soup is a great option when your child is feeling poorly as it's tasty, easy on the tummy and full of vital vitamins.

Serves: Four.

Ingredients

- 4 large carrots, peeled and sliced.

- 1 large potato, diced.

- 1 small onion, peeled and chopped.

- 2 tbsp chopped fresh parsley.

- 425ml vegetable stock or water.

- 1 tsp miso (a traditional Japanese seasoning).

- 200g broccoli or cabbage, chopped.

- 3 sticks celery, sliced.

- ½ bulb fennel, chopped.
- 2 unpeeled sweet potatoes, chopped.

Method

1 In a saucepan over medium heat, combine all the ingredients except the miso and allow to simmer for 50 minutes.

2 Whiz in a blender until smooth if you want a thick soup, or for a thinner soup simply strain out the vegetables and serve the broth.

3 Stir in the miso before serving.

Speedy Souping-Up Soup

If the sniffles have your family down, a bowl of this immune-boosting chicken soup will have you all up and about in no time!

The Magic of Turmeric

Turmeric isn't just used here to give the soup an interesting colour! This colourful spice has been used for hundreds of years, and is associated with loads of health benefits including…

- Reduced inflammation.
- Powerful antioxidant.
- Reduced risk of heart disease.
- Improved brain function.
- Helpful for arthritis.

This recipe makes seven servings.

Ingredients

- 1 tbsp extra virgin olive oil.
- 1 red pepper, chopped.
- 2 tsp ground turmeric.
- 3 cloves garlic.

- 150g raw wild rice.
- 3 tbsp fresh chopped basil.
- 1 cup – coconut milk, unsweetened.
- 4 cup – chicken broth, low sodium.
- 1 teaspoon – ginger root, fresh.
- 1 chopped – onion.
- 450g – chicken breast.

Method

1 Drizzle a large pan with olive oil and place on a medium heat.

2 Dice the chicken breast to manageable chunks and cook it in the pan for 3 minutes, stirring here and there.

3 Add the chopped onion and pepper to the chicken and stir it all together. Allow them to cook until the vegetables are tender.

4 Add the ginger, garlic (minced) and turmeric and stir until spread out evenly.

5 Add the rice and the chicken broth, and bring the liquid to a boil. Reduce the heat, cover the pot and allow it to simmer for a further 15 minutes.

6 Stir in the basil and coconut milk and allow to cook for another 3 minutes.

7 Serve warm, having first made sure the rice is cooked through.

Summing Up

- When your child is ill, a well-chosen meal can provide all the essential nutrients they need as well as being comforting.

- Nosebleeds may be reduced by foods rich in vitamins C and K.

- Children with acne can benefit from omega 3 essential oils which support skin health.

- In cases of earache, it can be helpful to cut down on mucus-forming and sugar-rich foods.

- When your child is feeling ill, soups are great because they're high in nutrients and really easy to eat.

- Foods high in iron are beneficial for anaemic conditions.

- Reducing intake of arginine-rich foods and boosting lysine-rich foods in the diet may help to reduce occurrence of cold sores.

- Beta carotene-rich foods may soothe eczema.

- Foods that reduce mucus production and boost immunity may help recovery from cold and flu.

Help List

Contact your child's GP or paediatrician if you have any concern about their diet or health. Helpful advice and products may also be found through the following organisations. All contact details are correct as of the time of publication.

Food and Nutrition Information and Support

British Association for Nutrition and Lifestyle Medicine (BANT)
www.bant.org.uk
As the professional body for nutritional therapists, BANT's website has a register of practitioners.

British Nutrition Foundation (BNF)
www.nutrition.org.uk
Delivers evidence-based information on food and nutrition in the context of health and lifestyle.

The Eatwell Guide
https://www.nhs.uk/live-well/eat-well/the-eatwell-guide/
The Eatwell Guide shows how much of what we eat overall should come from each food group to achieve a healthy, balanced diet.

The Food Commission
www.foodcomm.org.uk
An independent food watchdog.

Food Standards Agency (FSA)
www.food.gov.uk
Latest news and guidelines on a range of food issues, including labelling, allergies and food safety.

NutriCentre
www.nutricentre.com
enq@nutricentre.com
Offers advice on nutrition and sells a range of nutritional supplements.

The Vegan Society

www.vegansociety.com

Educational charity providing guidance on veganism, including information on raising infants and children on a vegan diet, soya infant formula, and baby and toddler recipes.

Vegetarian Society

www.vegsoc.org

Information for anyone following a meat-free diet, including a dedicated section for "Young Veggies".

Obesity Information and Support

Association for the Study of Obesity

www.aso.org.uk

The UK's foremost charitable organisation dedicated to the understanding, prevention and treatment of obesity.

Child Weight Management (Mytime Active)

www.mytimeactive.co.uk/cwm

Improving the wellbeing of its customers and their communities through well-managed, accessible and good value leisure, golf and health services. This organisation believes that everyone has the right to a healthy lifestyle, and wants people to feel the best they can.

National Obesity Forum

www.nationalobesityforum.org.uk

Raises awareness of impact of obesity on health. Includes information for children and families.

Weight-Loss Surgery Information

British Obesity Surgery Patient Association

www.bospa.org

T. 08456 02 04 46

BOSPA (British Obesity Surgery Patients Association) was launched in December 2003 to provide support and information to the thousands of patients in the UK for whom obesity surgery can provide an enormous benefit.

Weight Loss Surgery Information and Support

www.wlsinfo.org.uk

T. 0151 222 4737

Post: WLSinfo, 54 St James Street, Liverpool L1 0AB

Although this site is geared to adults, you can use it to access information and advice about children and to learn about what is involved in weight loss surgery. WLSinfo is a registered charity set up and run entirely by volunteers and maintained by donations from members. They are a leading source of support and guidance around weight loss surgery options in the UK.

Health and Wellbeing Information and Support

British Heart Foundation

www.bhf.org.uk

Research and campaign charity dedicated to improving heart health. Runs the Food4Thought initiative to tackle childhood obesity through diet and activity, and is campaigning for clearer food labelling.

Department of Health and Social Care

www.dh.gov.uk

Information on government health targets, plus guidance on obesity and nutritional programmes.

The Homeopathic Medical Association

www.the-hma.org

Register of qualified professional homeopaths, plus information on using homeopathy.

NHS Home

www.nhs.uk

A huge range of information on nutrition and lifestyle, including Live Well, Healthier Shopping and Health A-Z sections.

Allergy Information and Support

Allergy UK

www.allergyuk.org

www.allergyuk.org/information-and-advice/conditions-and-symptoms/586-types-of-food-intolerance

The UK's leading medical charity dealing with allergies. Offers a helpline, plus food alerts and a list of approved products. Their mission is to raise the profile of allergy at all levels, with a vision for everyone affected by allergy to receive the best possible care and support.

Resources for Schools and Teachers

The Caroline Walker Trust
www.cwt.org.uk
T. 01923 445374
Post: 22 Kindersley Way, Abbots Langley, Herts, WD5 0DQ
The charity produced guidelines, training materials and expert information on child nutrition needs in school and also on special needs nutrition. This organisation aims to help members of vulnerable groups who need assistance with nutrition and food. Their guidance is invaluable to anyone who cares for children.

Eating Disorders Information and Support

Anorexia & Bulimia Care
http://www.anorexiabulimiacare.org.uk
T. 03000 11 12 13 (Option 1 for sufferers, Option 2 for parents)
Advice and support for people with eating disorders and their families.

Beat – The UK's Eating Disorder Charity
https://www.beateatingdisorders.org.uk
A champion, guide and friend to anyone affected by eating disorders, giving individuals experiencing an eating disorder and their loved ones a place where they feel listened to, supported and empowered.

Hyperactivity Information and Support

Hyperactive Children's Support Group (HACSG)
www.hacsg.org.uk
Support group offering dietary approach to the problem of hyperactivity.